The Joy Codex

SCOT GORMAN

DEDICATION

This book is dedicated to all of those that have triumphed despite adversity and hardship. This book is also dedicated to those that still suffer, continue reading as there is relief on the way.

ACKNOWLEDGMENTS

Special thanks to my sister, mother, father, stepmother, family, and friends. I couldn't have done it without your support. Special thanks to the Wellness Center South in Lake Forest, CA it was their creative writing support group that gave me the confidence to put down into words what was in my head.

1 INTRODUCTION

Join me on this journey of self-discovery and spiritual reawakening. The Joy Codex is a set of principles I've developed and shared over my lifetime that have increased joy for me and others. Having joy shouldn't be a luxury. Joy should be simple enough to achieve that it can be done often, here is the key to increasing joy. This book is the story of my life and how I developed The Joy Codex, in order to heal my inner-child, and find joy in all things that have to do with life, love, and liberty. If you have lost your joy, never had it, or just need more joy in your life, you've found the right book.

What is joy? Why would you want to increase joy? The Miriam-Webster definition of joy is as follows: the emotion evoked by well-being, success, or good fortune or by the prospect of possessing what one desires, the expression or exhibition of such emotion, a state of happiness or felicity, a source or cause of delight. That sounds like something I want to increase in my life.

What to Expect

I'm a top down thinker and like to think in a chronological linear order, I've written this book in that manner. I felt it important to share my personal story, as that story is critical to the development of The Joy Codex. **Some of the names in this book have been changed to protect their privacy**. Additionally, there are worksheets included within the book and on-line that will get you deeply immersed in The Joy Codex methodology. It will be important for you to compete the worksheets as instructed. With that being said, let's jump right into the story.

2 IN THE BEGINNING

Trigger Alert, my story includes abuse in all forms, physical, emotional, and sexual along with alcohol and substance use. I've minimized or left out completely the most graphic details.

When did it all begin? Most people would say at conception; however, I'm going to go back even a bit further. It's important to understand the filters that I employ to interpret the world, it really is the foundation of the book and The Joy Codex.

Both my grandfathers were in the military, serving in WWII. My parents were born nine days apart in 1949, both ending up in Tustin, CA around the age of six. I don't know much about my family from this time other than the basics, they were so secretive back then. There are a few stories that have been shared with me, and I'm going to share them with you along with my story and how that relates to finding joy.

My grandparents lived one house apart, so my aunts and uncles all grew up together and were the within same age range. On the surface they appeared to be typical 1950's middle-class Southern California families.

Unfortunately, my maternal grandparent's family life was anything other than the typical personification of that era. What I do know is that my maternal grandmother, Estelle, was French Canadian, her parents, my great grandparents, were wealthy and living in Maine prior to the Great Depression. During the depression my great grandparents lost everything, causing my great grandparents to permanently abandon the family. My maternal grandmother ended up in an orphanage. These things greatly impacted Estelle's life and mine. Because my grandmother's family had lost everything, she became a hoarder, she always thought people were stealing from her and she had attachment issues.

My maternal grandfather Stanley was raised in Maine and was of English and Dutch descent. He was dealing with his own demons; alcohol and sexuality. My grandfather was a functioning alcoholic and had sexual urges for men, that he occasionally acted upon. I don't have too much more on him, he was a photographer in the war, a tool and die maker by trade. He was very intelligent and always corrected my grammar and would present me with words like "trepidation" asking me what it meant, although I had never heard the word before.

My paternal grandparent's family life was more in-line with what I imagine the 1950's represented. My paternal grandfather Michael was of Irish and German descent. He was captured when his submarine was torpedoed by the Japanese, there were only thirteen survivors, he spent about two years in a Japanese war camp. When he got out of the military he went to work for the State of California at the DMV. He was very stoic and didn't speak unless he had something to say.

My paternal grandmother Maxine was of French and Cherokee Indian descent. She was really the rock of my life, it's really a pleasure to write about her. She raised her five children and went to college at fifty-two and became a reference librarian for the County of Orange, CA. She was very patient and would always spend time explaining things.

My mother had a chaotic disorganized childhood and was damaged by the time she was aged 18. She started seeing my older half-brother's married father and got pregnant and had my older half-brother Dustin when she was 18; it was 1967. Two weeks after my half-brother was born, his father was working underneath the car when the jack slipped and crushed him. I'm not sure if other factors influenced my mother's unhappiness, I would imagine she had a difficult childhood based on her parents' issues.

My father; it appeared to me that my father had that 1950's childhood. I would imagine that it wasn't all rainbows and butterfly's though. I know that my grandfather was very though on him and didn't show affection and used corporal punishment freely. I have a hard time thinking of my grandparents as anything other than what I remember, wonderful loving people. My father went to college for horticulture from Humboldt State, and he also got a teaching credential, he was really smart. My mother stated that "the only time I ever saw him express joy was the day we found out I was pregnant with you."

I was born in March of 1969, a crazy time in the world, Kennedy had been assassinated a few years before, the Summer of Love was still partying on, civil unrest, Vietnam War, GREAT music, and an awakening social consciousness.

My mother's pregnancy with me didn't go as smoothly as her pregnancy with my brother Dustin. At some point in her pregnancy she developed Preeclampsia.

"Preeclampsia is a condition associated with high blood pressure during pregnancy. It is a serious complication of pregnancy characterized by the development of high blood pressure, edema (swelling), and protein in the urine." (www.emedicinehealth.com)

She also gained a great deal of weight quickly, so they put her on prescription weight loss medication. When I was born, I had the cord wrapped around my neck twice, and came out addicted to prescription diet pills. My mother claims that I cried non-stop for the first 3 months of my life as I also developed colic.

3 THE 1970'S

My sister Ali was born in 1970, my mother and father had been using drugs and drinking, my sister was often malnourished and listless as an infant and was often sickly. My maternal grandmother assisted with her care.

When I was 18 months old, my parents got a babysitter and they went out for the night. When they arrived home, they caught the babysitter sexually molesting both me and my brother, my parents had her prosecuted.

My mother and father eventually decided to separate in 1971. My mother moved to Garden Grove and my father finally ended up in northern California. I'm not fully clear about my mother's use of drugs and alcohol during this time, I know it was happening, but I don't know what she was taking.

A story my mother relayed to me, as she was attempting to teach my brother to speak, I learned to speak instead. I was two years younger than him, but I listened and watched what my mother was doing with my brother, and I started to speak full sentences very young and before my brother. I believe this is the reason I started testing at first year and second year college level for language and comprehension by fifth grade.

During this time, my aunt, my mother's sister, had to call the authorities because she found my mother in a state of over-dose from drug use.

A story that my mother told me; I was picked-up by the police for walking down the 22 Garden Grove Freeway in my pajamas while barefoot. When the police managed to get me home, my mother asked them which way I was going on the 22 Freeway, and they said east, which is towards my paternal grandmother's house. This was a lost time of neglect and abuse for my sister and me.

We left Garden Grove and my mother moved all of us to a very poor section of Santa Ana, this is when things went from bad to worse. She was still using alcohol and drugs; Barbiturates, I remember them being called reds and yellows, she did lots of LSD, Black Beauties and Cross-tops (AKA speed), Marijuana, and who knows what else she was ingesting. She had been driving a VW bug around 1974 and totaled the car and almost died, she was in so much pain. When she got out of the hospital, a neighbor offered her heroin to help with her pain and boy did it help at first.

I turned five in 1974, and this is when my memory of childhood really comes to life. I don't recall seeing my father often during this time, in fact I can only remember seeing him twice between two and seven years of age. He had an old Ford pick-up truck, it was white, and the driver's side door was yellow and dark. I have a visual in my head of the truck, with my sister sitting in the middle of the bench seat drinking beer out of her bottle; and yes, he put beer in her bottle. I remember that she was crying, and that I felt unhappy, now I would call it anxiety.

My mother was now heavily addicted to heroin, there were constant parties at her place. Our little apartment in Santa Ana had two bedrooms, my brother, sister, and I all shared a room. My brother and I shared a queen-sized bed and Ali had her own bed. My mother started dating a guy named Dudley, he was extremely violent. I have full length videos that play in my head of the many times he beat my mother to a bloody pulp.

One incident was very graphic. My half-brother Dustin was at his paternal grandparent's house, as he often was.

My mother, sister, and I went to spend the night at Dudley's and at some point they got into an altercation that led to him tossing her on to her back on the couch and literally punching her in the face full fisted and was pulling her hair out. I remember looking over at my sister and she was screaming, backing into a corner, I was looking at her and thinking "if she doesn't stop screaming Dudley will beat us too," as he had done so many times.

The next morning, Ali and I got out of bed before my mother and Dudley awoke, and we found my mother's purse in the middle of the street. Dudley had thrown her purse out so she couldn't get away from him, no keys!

The weirdest thing about the visual in my head of finding the purse in the middle of the street, is the amount of detail I remember. It was a brown leather purse indicative of the early 1970's, with a macramé strap. There was a cornflake dried on to the outside of her purse. I thought to myself, "that is really weird, how did a piece of cereal get stuck on her purse and how had it stayed stuck to the purse even after it had been tossed to the street."

This is about the time that I started to contemplate everything. I believe I was trying to make sense of the chaos; my memory really became over-active, I was trying to make sure that I knew what was coming and/or going, an attempt to avoid any threat real or perceived.

I was consistently in trouble during this time for having the runs in my pants, also known as diarrhea. I was so afraid all of the time. The courtyard to our second level apartment was fenced in and had a fenced yard that the units shared. I often hid behind that gate when I knew Dudley was coming over and hoped he wouldn't find me, all the while having the runs. It was awful.

I had a mother, but she was absent always, both physically and mentally due to drugs and alcohol. She would often go out and leave us alone in the apartment after we went to sleep. One time she lost her keys and tried to climb up to the second-floor window and fell and ruptured her spleen, all the while we were sleeping up in our room. She was loaded.

She had multiple sexual partners, along with her band of hippie friends. I remember one of the parties, all the adults were sitting in the living room in a circle, with us kids each sitting between an adult. Someone started playing the guitar and a joint was lit. As the joint went around, the adults put the joint to our lips and told us how to breathe the smoke in to our lungs and hold it as long as possible. They put us to bed and partied the night away, the next morning there were passed out, naked bodies on the living room floor and half-filled bottles of beer, which my sister and me gladly drank. I was five and this was the norm.

My sister and I were drinking alcohol, smoking, and being given mind-altering substances all by five.

For my sixth birthday my mother had me walk into a K-mart and try on a new pair of shoes. She told me to walk to the car and she would pay.

I remember thinking that "she didn't pay" and that "I was stealing these shoes." There were many times when my sister and I didn't have shoes, however I didn't want those stolen shoes.

The thing about stealing the shoes, my mother drilled into my sister and I's head that "God hates a thief and a liar."

One day I was walking to school, Edward Russell Elementary in Santa Ana and I was barefoot because I had no shoes. I got sent home and the school contacted my mother. I got beat for not having shoes. To this day I'm a shoe hoarder, I love shoes even though I don't wear them unless absolutely necessary. I prefer to go barefoot.

My father wasn't paying child support at the time and any cash my mom had went to drugs, we didn't really have much food and my mom rarely cooked. When she did cook, she made goulash and beef stroganoff. We always had cereal, hot dogs, snickers bars and sometimes milk, cheese, and butter.

If it weren't for the kindness of the Alta Dena milkman, we wouldn't have had milk, butter, cheese, or eggs, thank you Mr. Milkman! My mother stated later that she didn't have the money to pay for the food, so she thinks the milkman paid it out of his own pocket.

I always paid attention to my mother in the kitchen, which wasn't often. By the time I was five I could cook. I could fry eggs without breaking the yolk and I could use the oven, so I always cooked pot pies for my sister and me.

The times when there wasn't milk, we ate dry cereal or put water in the cereal, but there was always snickers bars. We weren't allowed to eat them, but we would sneak out to the kitchen in the early hours of the morning and steal a candy bar from the jar. We would turn the wall heater on and lay in front of it on the floor. Those were good memories of Ali, Dustin, and me.

My mother was in such a bad state that my sister and me spent a great deal of time at Orangewood, in my childhood it was known by the name Albert Sitton Home, it was a children's group home. I hated that place. Each time my mother totaled a car, or was otherwise unable to care for us, we ended up at Orangewood.

She started using it as a threat of punishment, that if we weren't good, she would call a taxi and send us to the home. One time, my mother acted like she called the taxi to come get us, and by chance a taxi was coming down the street, we ran and were scared, the taxi wasn't for us, only a coincidence.

I would imagine we were rambunctious as children, with one part-time parent, little food, violence, sexual abuse, physical abuse, and neglect. I certainly believe we were difficult. That doesn't condone their behavior, even if we were difficult, we didn't require corporal punishment.

Life for my sister and I was more difficult than for my older half-brother, as he spent copious amounts of time with his paternal grandparents. Although Ali and I spent time with our maternal and paternal grandparents, it wasn't enough to keep us out of harm's way. My grandmother Estelle was such a hoarder, that when we went over to her house it was over-whelming. There was stuff stacked to the ceiling and mushrooms growing out of the carpet. Since my mother and grandparents were at odds, we didn't spend too much time there.

It was November 1975 and we went to visit our maternal grandmother, whom we called Nana, both of my grandparents lived one house apart, so my sister and I went to Grandma Gorman's (GiGi) house. While we were there, she gave Ali and I a bunch of Christmas ornaments. As we were walking back to Nana's, we saw mom's VW Bug, and decided to decorate the inside of her car with the Christmas ornaments. We had left the doors on the car open so long we drained the battery.

Little did we know what was going on at Nana's. The gas company turned their gas off for non-payment, Nana decided she would go out and turn the gas back on, and she did. What she didn't know was that you only twist the valve part way to open/close. She turned that valve so far it shot off and natural gas was coming out of the gas meter, there was so much gas coming out of the pipe opening that there was a deafening whistle.

The neighbor from behind my grandparent's house heard the noise and popped up over the fence with a lit cigarette, my grandfather Stan was screaming at him to put it out. Nana always wore Mumu dresses; she fell over at the top of the backyard hill and rolled down the hill with her Mumu coming up around her waist.

My mother grabbed us and ran to the car, when she got in the car, she had to rip the Christmas decorations off the car and try to leave. The car wouldn't start, the battery was dead, and she made us push that car until she popped the clutch and got out of there. The police came and the fire department, they had to evacuate the block.

The authorities advised my Nana that there were services available to help her pay the gas bill if needed. She didn't need the money she forgot to pay it and couldn't have them turn it back on because she was a packrat and didn't want them in her house. This was indicative of our relationship with Nana and Grandpa.

When we weren't in the group home or with the grandparents, we were with our mother, which was most of the time. This lent itself to extended physical abuse, sexual abuse, and neglect. I was sexually abused until one month before I turned seven, I had prolonged abuse from multiple men, and a brother and sister team that lived in the next building downstairs. I remember she tried to force me to have sex with her and when I didn't or couldn't she slapped me across the face and when I tried to leave she locked me in a bedroom with her brother, were he proceeded to sexually abuse me. They threatened me with my life. I was so confused and afraid for my life.

I also had to watch as my sister was molested in her bed, while I was in my bed seeing this unfold. I really have vivid visual and emotional recall of these events, what I now know to be PTSD.

The apartment in Santa Ana was shabby, so Dudley came over to visit, and with another tenant, they proceeded to paint the building. The next morning Dustin, Ali, and I started playing in the left-over paint. When Dudley and my mother got up, they were so mad that we were stripped to our underwear and painted over our bodies with lead house paint, and then hosed off in the freezing overcast morning.

When we kids were in trouble, which was often, the adults in our lives used extreme punishment as a means of control. My mother would beat us with Hot Wheel tracks, I remember those orange tracks with the maroon connector. Those hard-plastic connectors when connected to the end of a Hot Wheel track really got moving fast, and when they connected with bare skin, the pain and welts were severe.

Dudley always immediately employed physical abuse, so my mother would try to mediate, as much as she could, without getting beat herself. She would make us stand in the corner in opposite rooms, and Dudley always came behind us after we were in the corner and shoved our heads into the corner so hard that our noses were hurt. We were told not to remove our noses from touching the corner walls. I can remember the smell of the paint, and how my breathe left moisture running down the wall. We had to stand for hours.

My father relayed a story that Dudley beat my sister, brother, and I so badly that we all ended up in the hospital.

My sister and I liked to play with matches and cigarettes and could often be seen down in the yard smoking my mother's cigarettes when she was drugged out. So many incidents over cigarettes.

On one occasion we were smoking my mother's cigarettes and got caught. My sister has a huge burn scar between two of her fingers where my mother put a lit cigarette out right at the base of the two fingers. For me she lit the stove and pit my hand in the flame.

Another time I was playing with matches and cigarettes and the carpet caught on fire, I really got it that time. It was always a bummer when my mother partied too hard and ran out of cigarettes because Ali and I liked them.

The first time I walked into the bathroom and saw my mom sitting on the closed toilet seat with a belt around her arm and a man with a needle in her arm, I was beaten and sent to my room for entering without knocking. I remember being confused about what I had seen and feared the needle after that incident.

Another time, my mother had a group of "friends" over for a party and I heard a bunch of commotion. The next thing I knew, my mother was lying in a bathtub, fully clothed with a cold shower running, someone said to me, "make sure she's breathing" and they all took off. I remember being scared and confused, unsure of what was coming next.

It was a 24 hour a day shit show. There was always talk in the family about my mother's behavior, so the times we were with the family it could be difficult for me to hear the conversation. They assumed I didn't understand, what they didn't know was that I already had advanced comprehension skills. They talked about courts and drugs and custody and yadah, yadah, yadah. Talk that never went anywhere.

My father went to court to get custody of my sister and me, but he walked in to court with a ponytail down to his waist, bare feet, and maybe a t-shirt, he didn't get custody that time. He also wasn't paying child support, so that also had an impact.

My father ended up paying all the unpaid child support. I was sitting in the living room at our apartment in Santa Ana in late 1975 and I overheard my mom talking to one of her friends that she was getting all this unpaid child support, over $3900.00 dollars, that is over $13,000.00 dollars in today's money. She bought a powder blue VW bug because I put sugar in the gas tank of her old maroon Volvo.

I later found out that my father had all the money, he was not paying the child support because he didn't want my mother using the money on drugs. He wanted that money to go to our care.

Boy do I have stories about my mom and cars. One time we were all riding down the 405 with my mother at the wheel and my Aunt Joan in the passenger seat. A police car pulled up behind her with his lights on, I remember looking out the back window of the VW and seeing those red round lights.

My mom was screaming at Aunt Joan to "eat the joint, eat the joint," I don't know who ended up eating it, but the cop breezed by and wasn't after them. They laughed and laughed.

Another time, my mother was driving in our neighborhood way faster than legal and as she came around the corner making a left on to our street, I was knocked over to the passenger door, which popped open. The window was open, so I grabbed the open-door panel. The door swung open and I was dragged all the way down the street with my feet flailing on the ground behind me as I held on looking down seeing the street beneath. I wasn't hurt only scared.

Another time, Dudley was driving my mother's VW, he was coming down our street and offered to let us stand on the running side boards with the doors closed. My sister and I stood on the outside of the car. He sped up and wouldn't slow down or let us off the car, so we jumped and ended up bloodied and bruised.

In early February 1976, my mother had recently totaled that new powder blue VW she bought with the child support money. She was in a cast on her left foot and walking with crutches.

My sister and I awoke early one morning to sneak a Snicker's bar and found my mother on the kitchen floor naked, just her cast and no crutches.

My sister and I tried to wake her up and she wouldn't. We noticed that she wasn't breathing, and we decided to put cough syrup in her mouth. I remember the syrup running down the side of her face as my sister held her head up and I poured.

My sister was crying and calling out for mom to "wake-up." I knew my paternal grandmothers' phone number, as I had called her a year before asking her how long to leave the potpies in the oven, she called the paramedics, we did have 911 back in those days, but I didn't know that.

They pronounced her dead, she had overdosed on heroin. My sister and I went to Orangewood, my brother had been with his grandparents. The interesting thing that came out of the investigation was that there wasn't anyone at the apartment other than my mother, sister, and me and they didn't find drugs or paraphernalia, they believe someone gave her the injection and left when she stopped breathing. I'm unsure of why my sister and I awoke when we did, we may have heard her hit the floor in the kitchen or that person leaving the house in a rush, this is all speculation on my part.

My sister and I rarely saw each other at Orangewood, I remember not having shoes, Ali remembers the overpowering smell of Pine Sol, to this day she makes comments about "food tastes like Pine Sol." One of the times we got to see each other through a chain-link fence and when they came to take us away, we grabbed each other's hands through the chain link fence and held on tight and cried to high heaven.

At the end of March 1976, my father finally came down from northern California to get custody of my sister and me. My birthday is at the end of March, so I remember spending my seventh birthday at my paternal grandparent's house and I received a lemon twist toy. That was also the first time that Ali and I flew on an airplane, Air California, they gave us cool pilots wings to wear!

We moved to a little town named Rough and Ready near Grass Valley. The little town only had a few hundred people, a little general store and a post office. We had a big yard with a stream running through the backyard where we could fish. It really does sound idyllic, and maybe under different circumstances it could have all worked out.

My father had a girl friend named Daisy, so we stepped into a new family and world, however, we were tremendously traumatized, so acclamation didn't come readily. My sister rarely spoke, I spoke for her, over the years I had become her surrogate father, cooking and speaking for her.

My father came from a childhood of spare the rod-spoil the child, we really didn't know him and who he was or what he was about. They had a little one-bedroom place with a partially enclosed patio. My father fully enclosed the patio, so we would have a room. Making a little hobbit door for us to access the room. Their bedroom window looked out over our new enclosed patio bedroom. I remember my father crouching to come through that little door into our room to punish us, we had accidently let a lamb die.

This time in my life feels like a mental fog, coming from the chaos of my mother and going to the chaos of my father.

My father and Daisy had lots of friends in the area, they were all hippies, lots of alcohol, drugs, and sex. One couple had a great house with a sauna and an above ground pool, everyone would pile into the sauna and jump into the pool at night. I also remember a friend of theirs that had a pet racoon, we loved that pet racoon. Rocky the racoon. My father and Daisy eventually decided to get married, that was in 1977. We eventually moved to Paradise, CA and settled into life.

There was lots of alcohol and marijuana and my father was a Clamper, or better known as the "Order of E Clampus Vitus." They were a drinking group and my father was a mean alcoholic. I don't remember the first time he beat me or the last for that matter.

I went from the frying pan into the fire when my father got custody.

In 1978 my father started an affair with another woman he worked with. He was rarely home, and we spent time with Daisy, she did the best she could under the circumstances.

She was young, only 22, and she was suddenly thrust into motherhood of two abused children, and a cheating alcoholic of a husband who was having an affair.

Daisy was going to break. She was going to school full time and we were often alone or had a babysitter. Daisy would read to us, The Hobbit and Lord of the Rings, I really enjoyed her reading. It made my mind race with thoughts and images as the words rolled off her tongue and escaped her lips.

Ali had been wetting herself for years and they kept punishing her each time. She was so afraid she would hide her soiled clothing.

The beatings from Daisy were usually with a wooden spoon on bare skin, those always hurt. I always hated when she got a really hearty wooden spoon with a thick handle and big scoop, those didn't break so easily so the beatings were prolonged and painful.

When Ali and I would get in to trouble during this time, our father would make us go pick a branch off a tree. He would strip the bark off the branch in front of us, and then whip us until we were welted.

One day a kid on the block got mad at me and followed me home wanting to fight. My father heard the altercation, and when I ran in to the house to tell him, he told me that I better win the fight because he would do worse to me than that kid would or could. I was more afraid of my father, so I didn't lose the fight. That bothers me. I really wish I didn't have to strike another kid in order not to get beat by my father.

This really sets the tone for my relationship with my father. I lived in constant fear, I was afraid for my life most of the time I spent with him.

In the summer of 1977, our mother, whom we thought dead, came to see us in Paradise. That was an emotionally draining event, and we begged to go with her when she left, and SHE WAS LONG GONE.

Late one night, I overheard Daisy on the phone screaming at someone, she said "he's my husband, you hear me!" Over and over. That was the end of that stepmom, and we had a new one on the way, Janice was her name!

My father and Janice got married in 1979, and shortly thereafter I had a new little half-brother, John. My little half-brother John had a completely different experience with my father. His childhood was free of the chaos and insanity that my father had allowed into my sister and my life. My father didn't use corporal punishment with my half-brother.

My stepmother Janice was very stable and no-nonsense, she also had a very difficult childhood. Janice did her best with my sister and me. We were well cared for and she loved us. She had a great sense of humor, very dry and to the point. I have an attachment to her and few others.

For me, there was lots of physical abuse, my father would back the car out of the garage, close the door, and beat me, he didn't want to beat me in the house, I guess that he didn't want my stepmother and Ali to watch.

He always explained after the fact why he beat me and make it a learning exercise, probably not the best way to discipline a ten-year-old. Those were bad beatings, and as always, I was afraid for my life.

Educationally, I always did well, although I thought I was stupid and often didn't know what to say. My father was always really hard on me about school. I almost failed the fifth grade, I had to do a state report, and I selected New York. I didn't know how to do the work and I was afraid to ask for help. The last week of school came and when I didn't turn anything in, the teacher called my father. Surprise, I got beat. I had the weekend to get the complete report done or fail. I pretty much copied out of the encyclopedia; I didn't get a good grade, but I passed.

By the time I was in middle school I was in the highest math class in the school and language and comprehension came easily. The one subject I love the most now, science, was at the bottom for me academically.

My father threatened me and beat me when my grades weren't good, I had to have great grades. He would berate me about not applying myself and that I was too smart for the grades I was getting, he would help me with math, but that was all.

My stepmother did most of the helping for homework, all except math.

One summer afternoon in 1979, I was playing in the driveway with my sister and my father was working in the garage. He came out and told me to "stop acting like a Swiss from San Francisco." I really was miffed, how would I know how to act like someone from Switzerland, I had never even met a Swiss person. I later understood that he meant is was acting gay. I guess I was gay even then and didn't know.

Goodbye seventies (also a reference to Yaz)! I'm deeply connected to music, and the memories that are connected to that music. Many flashbacks related to music.

4 THE 1980'S

Things were about to really change. It was 1981 and I overheard my father tell my stepmother that my paternal grandmother had sent a letter and that my mother had a new boyfriend in San Juan Capistrano. I recall them saying that they were "sure their mother and her new boyfriend were on drugs and that he was probably a drug dealer and that she was still strung out."

My mind went into overdrive, previously I had no idea where she was and now, I had an idea.

The next time my father and stepmother left the house, I picked up the telephone and placed a collect call to my mother in San Juan Capistrano. They didn't have her in San Juan Capistrano, but they did have her in San Clemente, wherever that was.

I told the operator that my name was Scot Gorman, but that wasn't my first name and my mother might not remember my name. When the operator said, "collect call from Scot Gorman" I blurted out my full name. My mother knew right away it was her son, I didn't need my full name. I was so elated. Ali and I continued to call our mother covertly and collect whenever possible.

It was a wonderful feeling talking to our mother. We longed for her and wanted to be with her, but our contact was a big secret.

In the summer of 1982, I hopped on a plane and spent the summer in Orange County with my paternal grandparents. My sister and I were really involved with my father's family because we spent summers with our grandparents. We never saw the other side of the family, our mother 's family.

That year I went alone to southern California. One day when my grandparents dropped me off at the theatre on El Toro Rd. I called my mom and wanted her to come to Lake Forest and view the movie too. My mother, and her boyfriend Rufus, wanted to come and get me and convinced me to ride down to San Clemente and see their place. It was a wonderful place a few steps from the sand.

I was so nervous and anxious that I wouldn't be back to the movie theatre in time and get caught. No one except my sister, my mother, my half-brother, Rufus, and I knew that we were all talking.

This is important to note because my father so disliked my mother that he had a hard time with me because I looked exactly like her. He would scream at me "you look just like your mother; she was a snake in the grass." If she was ever mentioned at the dinner table, he would slam his fist down on the dinner table so hard that the plates lifted off the table and slammed back down.

The sneaking around calling our mother was getting hard for everyone involved, especially our mother, she so wanted to help us but couldn't, we forbade her from calling our father or stepmother for any reason.

By early 1983 everything was coming to a head. Our stepmother Janice was chasing my sister Ali around with a broom trying to beat her because Ali had a smart mouth or wouldn't do her chores. Ali ran to a neighbor's house and called our mother, who immediately called our stepmom Janice. The "cat was outta the bag," and it was bad. I really thought my father would beat me to death. The relationship became more strained and I was very anxious.

There were good times too. We did a lot of camping and outdoors stuff, especially fishing. I would run a big front blade rototiller and till a huge backyard starting when I was ten. During the summer's that we spent with our father and stepmother, we gardened, went out to the hills and cut wood. I would chop and stack enough wood each summer, enough to get us through to the next summer. Our stepmother Janice always made holidays an event and I have vivid memories.

My sister and I spent the summer of 1983 in San Clemente. I had the benefit of spending the summer at Pepperdine University attending their computer camp. That was an excellent experience. I learned how to program in three languages and met some really cool people. We all stayed in the dorms on campus and each morning our camp counselor would come into our dorm room and sing "rise and shine and give God the glory, glory." This was the first time I felt encouraged and did well.

My mother had visitation rights, and her boyfriend Rufus was an engineer at the nuclear power plant, so they could afford an attorney. We spent Thanksgiving 1983 with my mother's entire family, it was so nice to re-meet my aunts, uncles, cousins, and grandparents I hadn't seen since 1976. Four days wasn't enough time, it went so fast and then we were back in the hell called Paradise.

I got caught stealing batteries from Pay-N-Sav and my father beat me so badly that I had bruises around my skull where he was punching me. He had taken me out into the backyard where he could beat me, I still have that memory burned into my brain. I had a school counselor, and I begged him not to turn my father in because I was afraid for my life, literally. And he didn't, that I know of, or nothing came of it until later.

School during this time was not good, Ali and I had serious trauma that continued when my father got custody. I had a hard time making friends and got called fag all the time.

I would have to get on the school bus and sit in the back with all the rowdy kids, they were older. They would spit their chew saliva all over my back. I also had to fight, fight, and fight. I was "called out" by other male students that thought I was an easy target. I never lost a fight, I couldn't, my father would do worse to me than any of these boys could, I never forgot that lesson.

During the 83/84 school year, my freshman year, I was so unhappy, I didn't know what depression was; but I'm sure now, that was depression.

By the end of the school year in 1984, there was no agreement that Ali and I would go see our mother that summer, we just assumed. When my father and stepmother said, "no you aren't going," all hell broke loose.

My mother and her boyfriend Rufus hired the attorney again and drove to Butte County to go to court. Our father came out of the courthouse and said that "your mother has backed me into a corner," and she could have permanent custody of my sister and me. We were so afraid of him, he convinced us to only go down to San Clemente for the summer and return back to Paradise. The courts had all of the reports from the school counselors where I had reported years of abuse, so he never beat me again.

Ali and I spent a delightful summer in San Clemente, we got to hang out with the Gorman's and my mother's side of the family. We made new friends in the neighborhood and got turned on to new music. Back in those days, Paradise was ten years behind the times. We loved the beach, the pier in San Clemente, and the music. Prince, Madonna, Culture Club, Yaz, Wham, Pat Benatar, U2, Don Henley; I could go on and on, that was truly the summer of music.

Ali and I also attended church with our mother, and we were both re-baptized into the Calvary Chapel Dana Point doctrine. We were baptized on Catalina Island that summer. We also went to Lake Powell with the Gorman clan and had a huge houseboat and ski boat; it was so nice to have that time with all the family.

That summer had to come to an end, and we had to go back to Paradise. We arrived back on September 4, 1984. I was so unhappy. This is when I first started seriously contemplating suicide, I wasn't allowed off our property unless I was going to school or with my father and stepmother. It was like I was on 24-hour lockdown when I wasn't at my mothers in the summer.

I started my sophomore year at Paradise High School, after spending a great summer in San Clemente with my mother. I stopped coming out of my room unless I had to go to school or was required to do something. I just wanted to die.

My sister Ali had been in secret discussions with my father and stepmother during that month of September deciding if they should let me go live with my mother. My sister agreed and on October 4, 1984 I arrived back down to San Clemente. My sister states "that was the hardest decision I ever had to make, and also the best decision I ever made."

When I received my school records from Paradise, there were handwritten notes all over my file, "Do NOT release any information to biological mother." There was a concerted effort on my fathers' part to keep us from our mother.

I can understand that, he did ask me through tears when I was 13, "why can't I have a chance, your mother was a horrible mother." I didn't want to hear him talk about my mother that way.

I was thinking that "my father had his chance and he fell short." For whatever reason, I had an expectation that when he got custody, he was going to be a knight on a white horse and rescue my sister and me. It certainly didn't work out that way. I'm saddened that my relationship with my father never developed. He did the best job he could at the time. He later made amends to me for the damage. I do love him.

He became disabled due to back surgeries and started taking opiates. He hasn't been the same since that time.

I did well that sophomore year, I was recommended to join the Academic Decathlon by an English teacher, and I did. I also joined the yearbook staff, made some friends, got called fag a lot, and went to church all the time.

I think this is the summer that I really started to struggle with my sexuality, I didn't know I was gay. I had girlfriends but there was always this heavy pull on my heart when I met a guy I really got on with.

There was a boy that was 15 and I was 14 and he was on the church camping trip on Catalina Island, I really liked him. I just didn't know what that meant.

I recall visiting my father for Christmas of 1985, and him making a statement that "all people with AIDS and gays should be thrown into camps and left to fend for themselves." Ryan White was in the news at the time and I said to my father "so you would throw young hemophiliacs into the camps?" He was so mad at me he walked away. I was thinking at the time, "what if I'm gay, is this what he would do to me."

I started working at the church, Calvary Chapel Capistrano Beach. I worked the sound board and duplicated tapes of the sermons and sold them after each sermon. I also started teaching bible studies on campus. I was pretty involved in the church.

The reason we were so involved in the church was that after my mother overdosed on heroin in 1976, she was baptized by Chuck Smith Sr. from Calvary Chapel Costa Mesa. So, it made sense that we attended Calvary Capistrano Beach as Chuck Smith Jr. lead Calvary Chapel Capistrano Beach.

Calvary Chapel Capistrano Beach was renowned for their music, Rick Founds was our church music leader, he is quite famous for his Christian music. I would lay in bed at night and listen to the musical tapes on headphones and cry that God would change me, change that feeling I didn't understand, homosexuality.

My mother and now stepdad Rufus, had purchased a new four-bedroom home in San Clemente on an acre. The development was so new, there weren't any busses, school or public, so I had to walk to school three and a half miles each way. They finally got a school bus out there the next year.

I started the tenth grade. Sophomore year was made more difficult by the fact that I was now living full time with my mother, Rufus, and my older half-brother. My mother was very cold and callous. She would play silent treatment when she was mad at me, I never knew why she was pissed, she was silent. Seriously, she wouldn't tell me why she was mad, I imagine this is when I became a mind-reader (sarcasm).

I made it through the tenth grade though! Summer was on! My sister came down that summer, it was a good summer. We didn't have any wheels, we would walk three miles each way to catch public transit so we could go to the mall, the beach, and all-over south Orange County. We were super mobile, it felt so good to have freedom and not be confined to a yard. We didn't care that it was hotter than hell and it was very hilly, we walked and rode everywhere.

As always, the good summer must come to an end. It was time for eleventh grade. I started my Junior year, and things weren't going well for me on an emotional level, I was extremely anxious and depressed. I had also just remembered all the sexual abuse I had experienced, up until that moment, those memories were repressed.

I was at a gathering at my brothers' apartment, he moved out early, so he had a place. He was renting a room from Angelica who also had three kids of her own. Angelica's kids were the same age group as Dustin, Ali, and me. It was like another little family; they were warm and inviting and we spent a great deal of time with them.

I digress, so, I'm at the gathering at my brothers, sitting on the living room floor listening to people talk and music play, all of a sudden I got really dizzy and then I was in this memory, it was like I wasn't at the gathering, I was living in a particular moment that was being visually displayed in my brain, with all the emotion.

It was like a movie playing, and the emotions that came welled-up from deep down. I can't say what happened or how long I sat on the floor in my own world, this is all a blur, all but that movie that plays in my head.

When I finally told my mother about the sexual abuse, I was sitting at the end of her bed, she was always laying on her made bed, it was her living-room. I couldn't look at her, and I was sobbing, I was so ashamed that I had been repeatedly sexually molested. I probably should have gone into therapy at that point, but my mother didn't believe in psychology, God was the cure.

As I had mentioned, I was in eleventh grade and my chemistry teacher came into class on the first day of school and said, "I don't care whether you came to class or not because my paycheck is the same amount."

I took that literally and didn't attend class. My parents had bought me a freeway legal motor scooter to get around on, I had a job at K-mart after school, weekends, and summers. I had gas and spending money. I was often grounded from my motor scooter and would walk down to the beach to the Ole Hanson Beach Club and hang out rather than go to school.

I got expelled from San Clemente High School for not attending class, they found out that I was the one signing my excuse notes. My mother didn't want to be awoken one morning after my first absence from high school and she told me to write the note, so I did. When she finally signed an absence note in my junior year and they compared all the notes, and saw that I was failing all my classes, they called her in to the office.

I had to meet with the school district along with my parents. They wanted to know why I wasn't attending class, and I told them, "if my teacher doesn't care, why should I care?" They let me make the choice of staying at San Clemente High or go to school at Dana Hills High School in Dana Point, CA, so I went to Dana Hills.

During a particularly long silent treatment from my mother, months, I finally went to the medicine cabinet and swallowed all the acetaminophen tablets. When I started feeling like crap, I went and told Rufus and he took me to the emergency room.

They gave me Ipecac to make me throw-up. When my mother came to the hospital to take me home, she walked in to the hospital and said to me, "I loathe what you did" and I told the doctor to "kindly escort her out of the room" and that "I won't leave the hospital if she is in the car when I leave." In retrospect I'm not sure why they didn't place me in a behavioral health unit. There was no 72-hour hold.

I completely dropped out of school, went to work for Mission Pizza in San Juan Capistrano, worked at the church, and took a third job as a taxi dispatcher at night.

My best friend from Paradise came down and we got an apartment on Del Mar in San Clemente, it was awesome at first. I was 17.

When I went to leave the house permanently my mother chased me down the driveway telling me I didn't have her permission to move out, I laughed, and kept walking. Who did she think she was, my mother! If it wasn't for my job at the pizza parlor, my best friend and me wouldn't have eaten. If someone ordered a pizza and didn't pick it up, I got to take it home.

I decided to move back into my parents as my roommate situation wasn't going well. A month before I turned 18, I helped a friend move, Cara, from the church. She was separating from her husband. After all my hard work, she wanted to say thank you, so she offered to take me to brunch one weekend. She picked me up and we got on the 5 freeway south.

Just before we went over the boarder to Mexico, we stopped at an ATM and I got cash. What a crazy weekend, Cara was 26 and hot, and hell, I wasn't gay, not that I knew anyway.

We went to a strip club in Ensenada, that was an eye opener. We got a cheap motel room for the night and I was deflowered.

We met this wonderful retired American couple that invited us to their beach trailer in Mexico for conversation, drinks, food, and friendship. That ended up being a godsend, meeting them.

On the way home Sunday night, the head gasket blew on Cara's car in Mexico, we had no money, and I had two broken fingers. When the head gasket blew, I was halfway between Ensenada and Tijuana on a dark highway. I had to pee from all the beer, so I ran off into the dark and tripped and busted those two fingers. We took a towel from her car and tied it off around my neck to make a sling for my arm. We had to cross the highway and hitchhike in Mexico back down to that American couple we met.

They lent us money and we got a hotel room in Ensenada; it was about midnight. I had to call Rufus and ask him to help us get out of Mexico, he met us at Papa's and Beer for drinks. He paid to have her car towed to the U.S. boarder and then towed to home.

I moved into Cara's place not long after that weekend. And Cara was now my girlfriend. She was such a delightful person to be with and around, she was beautiful, energetic, intelligent, industrious and best of all, she was mine.

I sat for the GED in October of 1987, I didn't complete the math portion, so I didn't graduate. They did grade my other sections and those scores counted. I received the following scores, as a Percentile Rank for the US, Social Studies was 72%, Science was 96%, Interpreting Literature and Arts was 87%.

Those scores were so good, they explained that the score wasn't a grade score, it was a score that measured how well I had done compared to other students, I was in the top 1% for science and the top 2% for literature and art.

The school administrators attempted to convince me to stay in school, I seriously thought I might. Ultimately, I had to decline, my situation didn't warrant high school until I was 20.

Cara got a job in Beverly Hills, so we moved to Hollywood. I loved it, I was now an adult and REM was playing on the radio. My girlfriend bought a new VW Cabriolet Wolfsburg Edition, I loved riding around LA in that car with the top down. I got a job at the same place as my girlfriend.

Emotionally I felt like a pinball bouncing off this and that without much direction or intention. I was feeling over-whelmed because of the battle that was going on internally over my sexuality and I didn't know what to do next.

I decided that I wouldn't change anything until I was clearer. Everything was going well. We didn't do drugs and we rarely drank. She always called me "pinche maricon," and I asked her what that meant, and she said, "it meant fucking butterfly, or faggot," little did she know. But she was about to find out.

She didn't like doing our laundry at the laundry mat in Hollywood because she thought those machines were dirty. So, we had to do our laundry over on Fountain Avenue in West Hollywood. There was this guy there that kept looking at me, and Cara noticed it and pointed it out. When she was loading the car, he came over and slipped his number in my hand. "That was a that," as they say.

I started to see this guy, and I never told Cara. I kept a journal in my closet that she found and called my mother and told her I was gay. I was devastated. My mother cried and cried that she was never going to have a grandchild from me, and she was correct.

Cara and I split, although, we still shared our 1930's Hollywood apartment, there was a big living room and sperate dining room, so I started sleeping on the floor in the dining room. She eventually told me to leave and I did. I found out later that she didn't want me to leave she was just mad. To this day I can't locate her.

I bounced around West Hollywood and LA for about a year, spending two nights a week at Studio One in West Hollywood, at the 18 and over gay bar. That was my one bit of respite from my inner turmoil with sexuality.

I was so ashamed of being gay, the church/religion and society frowned upon homosexuality, it was the 1980's and HIV/AIDS had stoked the flames of homophobia. It didn't help that my entire family was actively Catholic or Christian.

The church had spent years brainwashing me that homosexuality was a sin and I was going to hell and that there was no place for me in the church.

I ended up getting an apartment in West Hollywood with my best friend from Paradise again. I worked at the Broadway Beverly Center in Men's Furnishings and my best friend worked at Bullocks. We spent most nights at Revolver, I loved that bar. We eventually ran out of money and couldn't pay the rent and lost our jobs.

5 THE 1990'S

I couldn't return to my mother's, so I ended up moving in with some friends I knew from Paradise that moved to Orange County, CA. We lived in Laguna Nigel; I was such a mess. I started to have many more flashbacks and on one occasion they asked me what was wrong, and I said I didn't know. I was so anxious that at times I would be talking to the female roommate and gibberish would come out of my mouth.

The first time that happened, we were chatting and suddenly, strange sounds were coming out of my mouth and they weren't words. My female roommate looked at me with her head cocked and a questioning look on her face. I tried to speak again and more gibberish, I got so scared I started to cry, I couldn't speak, I couldn't communicate. It passed within 20 more seconds. I was afraid that I was going to lose my ability to speak for good. I later learned that I was having a panic attack.

I was working at the time, and I met this guy over the 900 numbers, yes that is how we did it back then, we didn't have the internet. His name was Dallas and he lived in Corona del Mar, CA. He said he was 26, I was 19 going on 20, and we started dating.

I had stopped drinking again by this time and was really bothered that Dallas would come home from work and do a shot of tequila. It brought up all the feelings I had about my mother and fathers abuse.

I acquiesced and started drinking with him. I also started noticing little things, he would be up late at night, he needed sleeping pills, and he drank a ton to sleep. I didn't know that he was doing drugs. When I found out, I started doing cocaine with him.

We both worked and were functional. He was actually 32, I found that out by being a snoop, I came across an old ID of his. I confronted him after days of inner turmoil and the worst anxiety. He said, "I didn't think you would like me if you knew I was 32 and I do look so young after all."

Dallas was from a prominent Texas family, with a long history in politics. His dad had been a state senator, his mother came from a prominent ranching family. They had a 10,000 acre ranch in Texas, we decided to spend Christmas there in 1990 or 1991. There was even an old ranch manager to manage the ranch.

When we arrived in Texas, we stayed with his friends, about three hours from the ranch. Dallas was acting really weird and spending lots of time in the bathroom. I asked him if he was doing coke and he said "no." There was a weird white powder on the back of the toilet bowel lid, it had a bad taste, nothing numbing like cocaine. I couldn't figure out what he was doing that night.

We ended up heading out to the ranch with his friends, we got out to the ranch after dark, and the tradition was you had to do a shot of tequila as you passed over each cattle guard. I was hammered by the time we got the ranch house and ridding on the hood of the car.

The next morning, the old ranch manager came into the main ranch house where we were sleeping. Dallas didn't want him to see us sleeping in the same bed, so he jumped out of bed and put on a pair of shorts. Dallas was not comfortable with his family knowing he was gay. I jumped out of bed and put my jeans on, which Dallas had been wearing the night before. I found a little tiny zip bag with white powder. I asked him what it was, and he said "speed," I said "Crystal," he said "yes." I was so upset that he had been lying to me, so blatantly, I couldn't believe it, I was devastated.

I told him "I am flying back to California immediately," he told me "to calm down" and said to me to "take this pill, it is like a Valium." It wasn't Valium it was Rohypnol, the date rape drug.

That drug was so strong that I couldn't walk or talk, Dallas told me "you better do a line of speed" as there were more guests coming to the ranch, and "you need to clean it up, you can't be hanging off door jams trying to stay standing." I did it, and it hurt so bad. My nose burned, but I was awake and alert. We entertained our guests.

We finally arrived home together after our time in Texas, and continued to do drugs, drink, and work.

It was about this time that I started taking the medication Prozac and started seeing a therapist in Laguna Beach. One of the pearls of wisdom from my sessions was that I was like a piece of luggage on a train. I wouldn't want to toss the luggage out without first taking a moment to see if there was anything of value within the luggage. "Gold" as she put it. I had to be diligent about my life and not dismiss all my experiences just to avoid the painful ones.

It occurred to me that I didn't have to condone or approve of the things that had transpired when I was a child, and at the same time understand that those things shaped my personality and made me who I was. I knew for me, that total acceptance and love for myself meant that I wouldn't change or erase my past. To be fair, it has taken me years to get anywhere near to actualizing self-acceptance and self-love.

I started feeling very creative and started writing and oil painting. Writing has been an excellent creative outlet, I'm always amazed when I go back and re-read something I'd written from this time in my life, I never thought it was any good. I suppose being an ENFP, I should've accepted that I could write. I was extremely hard on myself at that time, debilitating perfectionism at its best.

My mother was a prolific oil painter, so I always sat and watched her when I was a teenager, studying her use of pallet, brush, and technique. I enjoyed painting and was told by many that I had talent. I haven't painted for years; writing has really been my primary creative outlet.

I learned a great deal from Dallas, he was determined, articulate, professional, organized, spiritual in a non-religious way, kind, and a dear friend.

We traveled around the west coast, hopping in the car and driving to Mexico for the weekend, Mono Lake, skiing in Mammoth, trips to Texas, we were always doing interesting cool things.

Dallas had an antique spinet piano; he played and sang very well. Our general routine when not out and about, was to get some cocaine, alcohol, and cigarettes on a Friday night, listen to music and he would also play the piano and sing songs from artists like Joni Mitchell.

I believe this is where I started to experience some real joy in life, I was gay, I was living with my partner, I was working, a window into "normalcy" and what was possible.

There was still something missing though, and through therapy and long hours of contemplation I determined that I was still searching for something. I only had moments of joy; anxiety was my primary emotion.

I found it impossible to be a warm emotional communicative partner. I was even afraid to do something as simple was reach out and touch Dallas while we were sleeping. Physical touch was painful, to give and receive. Dallas was also noncommunicative and not affectionate.

Sharing my emotional needs was not going to happen, hell, I didn't even know I had emotional needs at that time.

I had to finish my GED so in 1992 I went back to complete the math portion; I was supposed to graduate in 1987 but only made it through the tenth grade. I had to pass the mathematics test, and I hadn't done much educationally after I dropped out from high school. I did start attending community college taking sociology and psychology courses, and I eventually quit.

I did pass the math portion with a pitiful Percentile Rank for the US of 42%, such a fall from being in the highest math classes to barley passing. I was finally a high school graduate five years late.

It was during this time that I lost my job which added undue stress to our relationship and my emotional state. This is also about the time that Dallas had invited a random guy from a 900 line over one night for a three way, I tried, but I couldn't. I really wanted to be with my partner, I loved him, both of us had an issue expressing that love.

Even though I really loved him, I could never express those feelings, I was afraid. I had never seen love demonstrated and was afraid of rejection.

By the end of 1992, I was doing my thing with my friends and he was doing the same. When I found a sexual partner at the Boom Boom Room in Laguna Beach, CA and we continued to see each other, I knew that was my queue to exit at the side door, I didn't want to stay in an empty relationship with Dallas.

I landed a new job at a thermoplastic resin manufacturer in customer service and moved out and got my own place in Costa Mesa, CA in January of 1993 on Magnolia Street. I was single and living alone. I felt such a sense of accomplishment and a bit of trepidation.

I enjoyed my new position; I gained some self-confidence. I was quickly learning that being confident, concise, positive, and always having a smile was a recipe for success.

I was very comfortable with customers over the phone and face-to-face and started traveling to see clients with each territory's sales manager.

I did well, I travelled as much as possible for work and personally. I had the pleasure of traveling to Italy, Switzerland, and France with the ski club I had joined. To this day Firenze (Florence), Italy is my favorite city.

That first trip to Europe was like a fairy tale. I found the only gay bar in Florence, that took forever, as the bar was unmarked and hidden. I had to watch other guys that I thought might be gay and see which door they all kept knocking on and entering. Resourcefulness!

I met this gorgeous 30-year-old Italian bank vice-president and went home with him, to his fabulous high rise on the River Arno.

The next morning, he asked me to stay, I said "I can't, I have plans to climb Giotto's Campanile with the ski club." He repeated himself again, this time asking me to "stay in Italy for good." I really contemplated staying, but knew I couldn't, because I knew I had to remain true to myself, my freedom, and my principles. I had an excellent job and life in California after all, that was what I told myself.

I flew back to California at the end of my vacation and resumed the life.

I was really struggling with depression and anxiety but didn't know that was the problem. I stopped taking medication and stopped therapy. I was going out four and five nights a week to the gay bar and drinking to socialize and meet sexual partners. I just had to buck it up and move forward.

The alcohol in combination with the speed I was snorting meant that my emotions were out of whack 24/7. I didn't have any control or understanding of the seesaw that was going on in my head and heart. If I wasn't going out to the bar, I was meeting up with friends and enjoying the wine.

I went back to community college and continued taking psychology courses and developed a keen interest in behavior. I was so curios about why people did what they did. What drives behavior? I had a million questions. I dropped out again though as my night life was more important.

I had already started thinking about how negative my parents had been and started altering my behavior so that I wasn't a negative person. Years before while I had been working at Mission Pizza, an older co-worker came through the door after delivering a pizza and I was at the register with a big smile on my face. He thanked me for always being positive and having a smile on my face. That stuck with me.

In retrospect, being a people pleaser was my survival mechanism for this time in my life. I had to smile, be positive, have integrity, be good at everything and try to make everyone happy; an impossible task.

I eventually moved back in with my parents in San Clemente and commuted to Costa Mesa for work. I couldn't afford my rent if I was going to go out every night of the week.

This was an important time in my life, the attachment that I felt with my mother was changing in a good way. I continued to actively read and study psychology on my own time. I often purchased college textbooks and even treatment books for my own psychological maladies. Not with the intent to fix myself, but to understand deeply.

My mother was fun to be around when we were out or had guests over. She was always warm and inviting and the life of the party. People loved her.

It was around this time that I decided to study attachment theory that had been developed by John Bowlby and Mary Ainsworth. Mary Ainsworth identified three primary attachment styles. Secure (type B), insecure avoidant (type A), and insecure ambivalent/resistant (type C). A fourth attachment style, disorganized was later identified.

I decided that my attachment style was disorganized. All the abuse during my early formative years meant that I was afraid to be soothed by my parents, they were supposed to care for me, meet my needs, and keep my safe, and they were the ones that either harmed me or allowed me to be harmed.

I learned how to detach from my suffering, like disconnected head, that feeling you get when you take cold medication.

I remember that it was better for me to remain as invisible as possible to stay safe, children were to be seen and not heard. My father always made that statement "children are to be seen and not heard" and my childhood was lived in that manner. As an adult it was difficult to overcome that disposition.

Living with my mother and stepfather Rufus during this time in my life was a positive experience and I continued to develop a relationship and attachment to my mother and Rufus.

I believe I was a distraction that they liked; I met their needs at the time. If I was there and available, they spent more time with me and less time on each other.

They fought constantly, screaming and yelling at each other all the time. They spoke to each other with such contempt that it was uncomfortable.

I thought I was so well evolved by this point in my life, that when they would fight, I would try to referee. Pointing out that one person was talking over another, something was said with the intent to hurt, or they were off the subject and on to another tangent. I finally realized that they had a codependent relationship with one another, and I was now a part of that, becoming codependent on them and their drama.

This is when I met boyfriend number two. We met under less than ideal circumstances. We met at the Boom Boom Room in Laguna Beach on a Sunday afternoon beer bust. I had been doing crystal along with a friend. Boyfriend number two was also doing crystal. Two kindred spirits. We immediately hooked-up and were inseparable.

We eventually moved to a fabulous ocean view apartment in Laguna Beach. We spent most work nights out with friends. The weekends were always going out. Friday, Saturday, and Sunday were whirlwinds of activity that included excessive amounts of alcohol and crystal.

This time is like a black hole in my life. The partying was non-stop. We would need to use speed to get to work each day and I did speed at work to make it through the day, just not to fall asleep at my desk.

He had an issue remaining faithful and along with the addiction to alcohol and crystal, I decided to leave. I didn't leave because of the alcohol and drug use, although that had a great deal to do with the demise of the relationship. I was still in search of the perfect relationship, whatever that meant.

I was expecting a partner that was going to sweep me off my feet, be romantic, monogamous, honest, integrous, sensitive, and intelligent with a great sense of hunor. Those requirements weren't aligned with my consumption of alcohol though. So, it was time to move-on.

I started working for an international relocation company in Corporate Services and moved to Belmont Shore in Long Beach, CA.

I had a little one-bedroom apartment four buildings from the sand. I stopped using drugs, I decided they were bad and not conducive to my well-being. Alcohol was okay though.

I was a few doorsteps down from Club Ripples, my favorite gay bar. I spent most every evening there as they had things going on during the work week. I was also in attendance most weekends. Thank you, John and Larry, for some of the best times of my life.

Work was going well; it was here that I started creating country guides for the executives and their families that were moving to a new country for work. I also started thinking about process improvement and repeatability.

During this time, I was contacted by a recruiter to interview for a position in downtown Los Angeles with a manufacturer of plastic cards, think credit cards, store credit cards, players cards, and room keys.

I became the manager of a team of customer service representatives.

6 THE 2000'S

While at this company, I learned to develop, create, write, and train team members to a set of ISO standards. ISO stands for the International Organization of Standards. My company was in the process of becoming ISO certified.

I had been exposed to ISO standards in my previous position with the thermoplastic resin manufacturer but hadn't had the exposure of creating the documents.

Creating standard operating procedures (SOP's) was difficult at first. Once I understood the format and purpose, it became easier and pleasant. I thoroughly enjoy writing procedures today.

Through becoming ISO certified as a manufacturer, I also learned about complaints and corrective action. These are themes that followed me through my career.

The computer system that we were using to enter orders was a DOS based program. The steps required to create a work order included retyping the build of the plastic card on four different pages, we didn't have cut and paste.

As a result, there were many remakes. The DOS system we were using didn't have any intelligence, it was really an accounting system with a lackluster add-on for work orders.

I spoke with the vice-president of the company about the problem and he gave me $100,000 ($160,000 in 2019) and a developer to create a custom solution; as none existed.

By the time the developer and I were done, we had an Access database that was menu driven and secure.

I created a nomenclature for each card that had intelligence. I could look at a card nomenclature and know exactly how that card was built. This allowed us to create bills of material that used specific raw materials, allocated those raw materials to a specific job, lot-control, and corrective actions for complaints.

The entire Los Angeles location was using the database with such success that the company spent millions to develop a complete custom solution using the access database as the roadmap. That custom solution ran the entire company at all locations.

My management style was open and encouraging and I wanted to see my subordinates succeed. Many of the people I hired were promoted out of my department.

I would say I was happy during this time, even though I had an enormous amount of anxiety. I lived alone again, I could park my car on Friday night and not need to drive again until Monday morning. Everything is walkable on the Shore. I had lots of friends and partners but found it difficult to connect on a deeper level.

I had a friend give me a hit of ecstasy on Saturday evening after a day of drinking at the marina. Ecstasy was the new drug, and I was taking part.

I met my third boyfriend during this time at Rage in West Hollywood, we were both rolling on ecstasy. Two weeks after we met, I left for Europe for three weeks. He ended up surprising me and appeared at Charles de Gaulle airport in Paris where I had three days left at the end of my trip. We were inseparable from the start.

He wanted to go back to school and complete his degree in psychology. I was in total support of this initiative.

My anxiety was getting the better of me, I'm sure the alcohol and ecstasy didn't help. I was in the process of being promoted at work and would be spending four months at corporate in Denver.

I was at my office in Los Angeles and my anxiety was so bad that I called my boss and told him I wouldn't be coming to Denver and I was quitting my job. I got up and left the office midday and went home.

When I got home my boss called and said that I was coming to Denver and I couldn't quit. I'm so thankful he did that. He asked me what the hell my problem was and to make sure I was in the office on Monday.

My boyfriend recommended that I get on medication for generalized anxiety disorder (GAD). He was correct. I had never known what it felt like to have normal anxiety. For me everything was always the worst possible outcome. I catastrophized everything in my life. I've heard anxiety described as "future tripping" I like to call it "mind fucking." What if, what if, what if; and could of, should of, would of thinking.

I would have an issue and think of all the possible outcomes and then I would start over in my head, rethinking all the possible outcomes and what I would do to mitigate any catastrophe.

The medication put me on the same playing field as those that didn't require medication. I didn't stop having anxiety, it was more manageable. Anxiety has served mankind well, and it is an important survival mechanism when it isn't running out of control.

I did take the promotion and moved to Las Vegas after four months in Denver. I was working out of my home office and responsible for sales of plastic cards to the national gaming industry along with accounts in Nevada and Arizona that weren't gaming related.

It was difficult adjusting to work without subordinates, not being in the office and not seeing a tangible product.

Although I was successful and grew the territory sales by 28% that year, I wanted to manage people again. I quit that job finally.

I went to work for a company in Chatsworth, CA that manufactured personal care products. If you have purchased lotion, shampoo, conditioner, sun block, wrinkle cream, or salt and sugar scrubs, then you have purchased products made by this company. They are known as fillers.

This position was the most difficult to comprehend and learn well. I had a team of planners that worked for me; they were responsible for bringing in all the components and raws to meet the order requirements of the customer.

The components and raws came from many different suppliers, all with different lead times. We were using an ERP system, enterprise resource planning.

We were going through an upgrade of our system and I was tasked with assisting that effort. In addition to the upgrade, our system didn't do a great job of handling complaints from customers. I developed the procedure and the module of the software that handled complaints and corrective actions.

I was commuting to Chatsworth for the work week and back to home in Las Vegas for the weekends.

I was recruited again, and I took another position with a large furniture manufacturer in Culver City and moved to Culver City, CA. Moving boyfriend number three back to California from Las Vegas.

I was managing three departments and had about 15 direct subordinates. This company was also going through an upgrade of their computer systems, so I was very actively involved in all aspects of the upgrade including writing test scripts to ensure the software was working as planned and designed; and testing.

As my responsibility increased so did my salary and bonus. I had been doing well professionally and this became my identity. As long as I was doing well at work, my personal life was incidental.

I had included benzodiazepines with my SSRI for generalized anxiety along with alcohol. I worked many hours, I had the furniture markets in North Carolina, Mississippi and Las Vegas twice a year and as long as I was working, I was able to put one foot in front of the other.

The evenings and weekends were difficult, as I was severely depressed in addition to having anxiety. My relationship wasn't that good either, so I drank alcohol most nights.

I was receiving 180 benzodiazepines per month at 4mg. In retrospect, that was a lot of medication.

My second suicide attempt entailed alcohol and those pills. I was sitting in a grocery store parking lot when I swallowed those pills. I awoke 4 days later in ICU. After I was released, I went home and picked up where I left off. I didn't attend any counseling or support groups and my life continued in the same manner.

I had always loved automobiles, and as the lease was up on my Audi A4, I decided to lease an Audi A6. That was my feel-good tool after the suicide attempt. I always had a car in mind, something that I was working towards. Having a goal for a new car was the only thing keeping me going.

I accepted a new job with a start-up in Irvine and moved back to Corona del Mar. The start-up folded due to shenanigans by the owner with investors' money.

I was jobless. I couldn't believe it. My partner encouraged me to take the year off and get therapy, which I did. The therapy was helpful, and I learned a great deal about myself.

I also went back to school majoring in psychology, completing all but my capstone/senior project and some general education requirements.

This is when my relationship really started the long slow slide to termination. There was infidelity and dishonesty on his part.

I attempted suicide again, this time I took all 180 benzodiazepine pills and 30 prescription sleeping pills and quickly washed them down with vodka martinis.

I was in ICU for 4 days and my partner told me I couldn't come home unless I went to alcohol treatment. I was also placed on a psychiatric hold. I went to treatment in Laguna Beach, as it was close to home and the treatment center had a gay group for gay people. I was in therapy for about nine months after I left treatment.

I became so depressed that I was diagnosed with major depressive disorder (MDD). It wasn't the alcohol, because I was sober, more medication was ordered.

This was the first time in our relationship that I wasn't the primary earner in the family, and his treatment of me decreased during this time. I decided that I needed to go back to work so that I wasn't treated poorly and marginalized. At least when I was working, I had a positive identity for myself.

When I lived in Las Vegas previously I had purchased a home and rented it out when I moved back to California. It was time to move back to Las Vegas.

I was hired by a fortune 50 pharmacy benefit manager (PBM) as a manager, with four supervisors, two ancillary staff and 120 customer service representatives reporting to me.

I had dotted line responsibility for 575 representatives, our location had 2200 employees. I also led the reward and recognition effort by the company at that site.

The company invested heavily in my career. They sent me to a week of training in Atlanta at Aubrey Daniels International (ADI) getting a certificate in performance management.

Through performance management I learned about behavior and what increases or decreases behavior. I had to identify the specific things a subordinate was doing by their behavior and decide if that was the behavior I wanted for that specific requirement. Once I was able to identify and measure behavior, I learned how to increase or decrease behavior through reinforcement, punishment or penalty.

The first thing that occurred to me was that my subordinates were doing what they were supposed to because they didn't want to be punished or penalized. This management style increases the desired behavior, but only the bare minimum.

Imagine that you have a manager that is nice, positive, friendly, and genuinely cares about you. However, each time that manager comes out of the office you turn away or try to look busy. This is management by negative reinforcement. You will do what you are supposed to in order to avoid that penalty or punishment, assuming it is coming, and only doing the bare minimum.

That was an eye-opener, I was negatively reinforcing my subordinates. I had all the rules and regulations for my subordinates and because of my experience with ISO certification, I had training rosters in their files to ensure I had documentation that they were trained and understood each rule.

I didn't like to terminate subordinates, but when I did, I had everything I needed, even with the union representative present. Aubrey Daniels taught me that I could've done more to encourage my employees and reduce attrition.

I fully embraced ADI and became the Las Vegas site champion for the program. This program has followed me to all future positions. Aubrey Daniels wrote the college textbook *Performance Management, Changing Behavior that Drives Organizational Effectiveness.* I own this book and refer to it often.

Some of the key things I learned, behavior is something that can be seen or heard and is repeatable and measurable. I learned how to build-in positive reinforcement for the specific behavior I wanted to increase and schedules of reinforcement. By use of operant conditioning I could increase or decrease behavior.

I was asked to participate in an exercise while at ADI. I would leave the room and the instructor would tell the class what he was going to get me to do, without ever speaking a word. He used a training clicker. If I heard the click, I was doing the correct thing, if the clicks stopped, I was doing the incorrect thing.

When I came back into the room I started walking forward and heard the clicks, I kept walking straight and the clicking stopped so I stopped. I turned right and left, no clicking. I walked back a couple of steps and got the clicks again. The instructor managed to get me to pick up a coffee cup off the table from one attendee and place it on the table across the room of another attendee; without a word.

Another example they used to demonstrate why reinforcement was so important was to have us imagine that we entered a room and switched on a light that didn't illuminate. You might switch that light on and off a couple of times, you would quickly stop that behavior as you weren't getting the result you expected. That behavior would extinguish through consequences.

It became evident that positive reinforcement via positive consequences increased the likelihood that we would turn that switch on again in the future.

Once I understood behavior in this context, I could start applying it to my personal life too. If there was a behavior I wanted to increase, I would need to understand what drove that behavior and reinforce that behavior.

I also went to six sigma greenbelt training, where I learned the five main concepts of six sigma; define, measure, analyze, implement, and control (DMAIC).

If you don't know what the problem is (define), how would you measure or analyze the problem or implement a process or procedure for improvement and control. This process is continuous as you are always measuring how well the process is working. If changes are required, you make those changes via the DMAIC process.

I also learned more about corrective action and root cause analysis, one of the tenets being ask why 5 times. The first answer to a question generally leads to additional questions to determine the true root cause of an issue.

This methodology can be applied to personal life too, not just the professional realm. I love to ask why.

The application of performance management along with six sigma methodology has come to define my management style.

Things were about to change in a major way. During 2008 and 2009 I had multiple surgeries on my left ankle and became addicted to pain pills. I finally left this company and moved to Chicago so that my partner could complete his Ph.D. in psychology. I was unemployed again.

7 THE 2010'S

I went to work for a large industrial and commercial plumbing manufacturer on the south side of Chicago as a customer service manager.

While living in Chicago, I needed more and more pain pills to make it through the month. I was taking Oxycodone, Roxycodone, and Dilaudid daily. This was unsustainable. I could never do heroin if I was cut off from the pain pills; which is the outcome for most. Heroin would've meant that I was a drug addict, not all the pills I was taking. I started methadone treatment.

My mother came out to Chicago to visit me, and it was a disaster, she was drunk most of the visit, breaking furniture and washing my clothing that had electronics in the pocket. She even left her purse on the airplane as she arrived in Chicago because she was drinking on the airplane.

I had been drinking with my mother and Rufus for years, they both encouraged drinking. I had been dealing with my mother's severe alcoholism since I lived in Belmont Shore. There were times that we would get tossed out of a bar on 2nd Street because she was so wasted.

Things were going well at the new job. Performance management came with me, and I implemented the program at my new position. I don't make that statement lightly. It takes a great deal of effort to define the behavior that leads to a successful business.

Simply saying, "hey good job" isn't enough to increase behavior. It takes a few months to implement the program well.

On the personal front, I had my Volvo car so I must be doing well. My partner and I had grown so far apart that we didn't sleep in the same bed anymore, I couldn't, my anxiety would become so increased when I tried to sleep in the same bed that I wouldn't sleep.

He graduated and we moved back to Long Beach, CA. I took a position as a software consultant within the software-as-a-service (SaaS) industry.

We finally broke-up and both moved to our own places. It was time for me to get my personal life in order, I wanted happiness and joy. I decided that it was time to get off methadone. The clinic wanted to cut me down by 1mg every two weeks, I was taking 170mg a day.

I had already been on methadone for about four years. I didn't want to stay on the medication for another five years. I took drastic measures; I don't recommend that others follow my lead. I decided to cut that time down to a month. I was off methadone; it was physically hard on my body and my psyche. It took more than four months before I really started to feel better.

I also started Cognitive Behavioral Therapy (CBT) and began the slow process of understanding how my thoughts and emotions affected my behavior. Therapy also increased my confidence.

I had about two years of sobriety, no alcohol and no substances. Previously I had stretches of nine months of sobriety here, a year there, but nothing long term. Once I was clean and clear from methadone, I thought I could drink alcohol again, as I hadn't been drinking for about a year.

I didn't spend much time with my mother and Rufus, the round trip from Long Beach to San Clemente was more than 100 miles; and that is too much time with weekend traffic.

During this time my mother slipped into a deep depression (undiagnosed) and drank alcohol to cope. She was in and out of the hospital in a coma, with kidney failure, and broken bones. This went on for years. My sister and I attempted to help my mother on numerous occasions, we tried to get her into a program. She almost went into treatment on numerous occasions.

The time my mother went into a coma, she had fallen and hit her head the previous week. A week and a half after the fall, Rufus was on his way to work and stepped over her as she laid on the floor and went to work for the day. My sister showed up to the parent's house during her lunch break to check on my mother and discovered she was non-responsive. They had to resuscitate her, and she was in that coma for about a month.

Her cognitive abilities were reduced, she had trouble speaking, remembering, and had difficulty with her motor control. Her brain had moved an inch and a half off center.

She did recover after a year and a half, I would bring her magazines that had the same image on either side, and she would have to find the differences. The other therapy that she was engaged in wasn't having much of an impact. It occurred to me that she was very visual, she was an oil painter after-all.

My thought process was that she would be using both sides of her brain by identifying the differences in the images. She had trouble speaking the differences at first, but she could point. She improved quickly and eventually returned to her normal.

Another time, Rufus was on his way to work and my mother was in the breakfast nook laid out backwards over the seat of a dining room chair, he left her there. Once again, my sister came to the rescue, my mother was in renal kidney failure from being left on the chair arched backwards, feet and hands touching the ground. She spent most of the day in that position. She had dried blood on her cheek and down the wall, poor sister, almost like when mother overdosed on heroin. She had to be resuscitated and was on dialysis for an extended period of time.

Rufus wasn't supportive of her getting help. She got a DUI and had to go through the DUI program in California, which at the time meant nine months of classes and support groups.

When my mother was doing heroin in the 1970's she acquired hepatitis C. After her overdose she didn't drink or do drugs. She didn't start drinking again until her dad died in the mid 1990's.

The alcohol destroyed her liver and she was ineligible for a liver transplant because she wouldn't stop drinking alcohol.

She was also having seizures when she drank, unbeknownst to the family. The doctors believe this is what was causing her to fall and become injured so often and so dramatically.

She finally was diagnosed with cirrhosis of the liver. Rufus continued to provide her with alcohol and medication she wasn't prescribed, getting them from Mexico. He was getting opiates, benzodiazepines, and muscle relaxers. I asked him to stop providing her illegal medication and alcohol and he said he couldn't, that my mother was mean to him. He was well aware that the alcohol and illegal medications were a sever harm to her liver.

When she was resuscitated with kidney failure, the doctors had tested her blood and they knew she had medication that hadn't been prescribed. They pulled Rufus aside with my sister present and told him that if she died on one those medications, he would be held liable and that he could no longer provide them. My sister and Rufus were separated and spoken to by the Orange County Sheriff's Department on two sperate occasions. Nothing ever came of those conversations just a warning.

My mother was so loaded all the time from the medication and alcohol he provided. I thought she was the one taking all this medication until I came over one weekend and noticed that Rufus was putting pills in her mouth and washing it down with a water bottle from her nightstand.

I didn't see any alcohol on my mother's nightstand, so I asked him what was in the water bottle, and he said, "I put vodka in her water bottles." I asked him what he was giving her, and he said "I am giving her a Soma" a strong muscle relaxer. I asked him "why?" I had taken those same muscle relaxers; I could see that she had lost all motor control. He told me that she couldn't take the medication herself, so he did it for her. I was so pissed-off I screamed at him again to stop trying to kill my mother.

I believe we tried to protect Rufus from his wrongdoing with my mother on many occasions. We felt sorry for him. I believe this is the reason he hasn't been charged with a crime.

She was difficult and she had to have her way. That didn't mean she should be provided with unprescribed narcotics and alcohol. I finally had enough and called the County of Orange and reported him for adult abuse, detailing the entire situation. They came out and saw her and she convinced them she was fine and didn't need help. She was so fearful of not having the alcohol and medications to numb herself. I feel that the county let her down.

She couldn't drive, she had a major car accident and received another DUI. This time she didn't have any alcohol in her system, but the medication was building up in her system because her liver couldn't process the medications. She also had elevated concentrations of ammonia in her brain. She spent six or nine months in jail and was clean and so very happy.

Getting away from Rufus really lifted her spirits. I thought that when she arrived home, she would remain clean and that Rufus would support that. He didn't. He stated to my sister "I asked your mother what was the one thing that she was most looking forward to now that she was out of jail. She said a glass of champagne."

I was still living in Long Beach and work was up in El Segundo, it was tough to get down to San Clemente to see my mother. And when I did, it was too difficult to deal with, I started drinking again, wine, a great deal of wine daily.

I was doing well at work, being a software consultant onboarding companies that used our software through Salesforce. I was also writing standard operating procedures for my department.

My mother's cirrhosis progressed to the point that she was given six months to live and was placed in home hospice. Six months stretched out into two and a half years.

During one of those weekends to San Clemente, Rufus and I took my sister to a concert at the Coach House as a birthday gift to my sister. Rufus was talking to some lady named Gladys and her brother, and he disappeared with them for most of the night. We didn't think much of it.

I was also back on opiates; I have been called a klutz most of my life. I'm always in a hurry and seem to get injured often. Adding alcohol to the mix is certainly a recipe for disaster. I broke my left elbow while on a camping trip with a gay camping organization I joined. The doctors gave me opiates. Shortly after the left elbowed healed, I broke my right elbow and wrists after falling down the steps to my sister's apartment. I was given more opiates. I knew I shouldn't take them. I was addicted again.

I was also on a camping trip with the gay camping group and fell and fractured my sternum, more opiates ordered. It was one mishap after another for me during this time.

Rufus was retired but was doing minimal consulting. He was allowed respite services every month. Once a month, he loaded my mother into the car and drove her to a nursing home for a week at a time. I thought this was good for my mother, if he was less stressed by her, he wouldn't be so nasty to her. He was an ass to her in her sickest moments.

He was also over-medicating her so she when she was at the nursing home she was medicated properly, she was coherent. I now think we should have let her stay in that nursing home. On numerous occasions the home hospice nurse had to warn and admonish him for over medicating her, telling him that if it continued, they would have to report him.

I was emotionally detached during the last six months of my mother's life. I had placed all my personal effects in storage, moved back in with my parents in San Clemente and worked from home to help take care of her.

She always liked to share her meds with me, so I started taking her oxycodone and morphine, it finally got to the point that if she was unable to take one, I would take it for her even stealing them. I was addicted again. Getting off opiates was three weeks of hell.

She finally passed, August 2017. The hospice team was very accurate about her passing time. They knew that she was going to pass within a week. Rufus left claiming he had a business meeting for the week. He wasn't even going to say goodbye to her, although she was catatonic. My sister made him say goodbye to her.

I was in the backyard gardening when she passed. My sister, aunt, and cousins were with her when she took her last breath.

My sister immediately came and got me, and I tried to give her mouth to mouth resuscitation to get her back. I didn't even know what I was thinking. I wanted her to pass at this point, she had bed sores that had opened to the bone and she was not cognitively aware, she was on drip morphine by this time.

I took her death harder than I initially thought I would. I have never been angry with my mother for her actions in the past. This time it was different, I was feeling abandoned, and there wasn't any need for her to be dead. If she would've made the choice to abstain from alcohol and prescription medicine that wasn't prescribed, she would've lived. I was angry with her. I thought "what was the point of saving her in 1976 from the heroin overdose if she didn't care about staying around for her kids and grandkids in the long run."

After the funeral I went back to the office in El Segundo, making the commute each day from San Clemente, about two hours each way on a good day. This time was well spent, I started thinking about what I wanted from life.

My mother was so much fun to be around, she always smiled, hugged everyone, and was warm and inviting. Holidays were the best, as my parents had the biggest house, all of the family always spent the holidays with us. During summers, there were always many barbeques at the house with all of Ali, Dustin, and my friends in attendance. My mother even invited my friends and co-workers to holidays if they didn't have any family.

I started looking for an apartment in L.A. It was December and Rufus invited my sister and I to dinner to meet a "special friend." It was midway through dinner that this woman accidently blurted out that she had met us previously, two years ago at Coach House. It all came crashing down at that moment. It was Gladys.

It is interesting to note that Gladys quizzed my sister when Rufus and I went to the bathroom. She wanted to know where Rufus disappeared to and what he was up to, my sister didn't say a word protecting Rufus. Little does Gladys know, we all went out shortly after my mom died and after a couple of cocktails, Rufus was lip-locked to a woman with long brown hair. He stayed lip locked to her that entire night. We actually thought this was the woman he had been seeing, as we knew he had another woman. It wasn't her, it was Gladys.

Rufus had been seeing this woman Gladys long before my mother died, buying her a Mercedes CLS550 and fixing her teeth. When I asked him why he was doing all this he stated, "she was helping me start my business." It seems odd to me that a man with an MBA and a PE (Professional Engineer) certification would need help from a woman that walked dogs and worked part-time at Nordstrom's. And a new Mercedes as payment, nice arrangement.

After my mother's death, the neighbors shared with my sister and I that they often saw this woman driving up and down my parent's street also parking in the driveway.

About six months before my mother passed, she claimed that a blonde woman had been in the room across the hall with Rufus hugging and kissing her. Rufus said my mother was crazy and imagining things. We now believe that this woman spent the night and my mother was absolutely lucid.

Two days after that dinner I went out and drank my sorrows away, on the way home I thought I was on a main thoroughfare street but was a on a very narrow car lined street.

I was speeding and came around a corner and slammed into the curb just barely missing cars. I totaled my Volvo, they cut me out of the car, and I was arrested for DUI.

I decided I needed help and checked myself into the hospital to detox from alcohol and then went to treatment. I have mixed emotions about the treatment center I selected, they were considered a dual diagnosis program, which means they handle cooccurring diagnosis, an addiction and psychological diagnosis. They didn't have any classes or specific groups that dealt with the psychological diagnosis.

I was sober until the day they released me, I left the treatment center and went directly to the liquor store and bought a handle of vodka.

Within the week I had attempted suicide and spent four days in the critical care unit while they tried to prevent damage to my kidney's. I was sent to the Behavioral Healthcare Unit (BHU) at Mission Hospital in Laguna Beach, I was placed on multiple holds and didn't get released until I had arranged to transfer to another inpatient treatment program.

The program I selected was also a dual diagnosis program, it was poorly run and managed and I left the program after 26 days. Within a week I had another suicide attempt and was back on the BHU in Laguna Beach. I was again placed on multiple holds and had to arrange for inpatient treatment before I could be released.

I chose to enter Casa Palmera in Del Mar, Ca. This is a true dual diagnosis program and I'm thankful that I was able to attend. They tailored a program to my specific needs and all services including meals were provided on-site, we left the facility for nature outings, beach time, and the anonymous support groups.

This program is by far the best that I've come across. I spent time each day in sessions specific to depression, anxiety, and PTSD. All the staff was incredibly knowledgeable. I was particularly impacted and learned the most from a particular Primary Care Coordinator, Ayesha Suneja, Ph.D. She was very kind and compassionate and was critical in my understanding of the application of the different elements and components of CBT/DBT. I'm forever in her debt.

I completed my time at Casa Palmera and moved into a gay sober-living house in the Hillcrest section of San Diego. Living in a sober living was an enjoyable experience and learning to live with 24 gay guys trying to remain clean and sober. Girl! That is all I'm going to say.

During this time Rufus cut all ties to the entire family, saying that he couldn't deal with our drinking. I find that statement interesting, considering he encouraged drinking. We would often go out at his request and drink.

I remained sober for six months when I made the choice to start drinking again, I thought I had everything handled. I had received a great deal of care and support while in San Diego. I concluded that I was an alcoholic because of the depression, anxiety, and PTSD, that drinking was the symptom. I still do believe this to be true. If I had been better at addressing the underlying issues rather than the symptoms, I would've remained sober.

July was leading to August, the one-year anniversary of my mother's death, I was unaware of the internal emotional upheaval that was just underneath the surface. I had another suicide attempt, this time having a heart attack and spending four days in CICU. The interesting thing about this suicide attempt was that I wasn't emotional about it, I was done.

It was very calming to get to the point that death was better than the emotional pain I was feeling. I went back to the BHU in Laguna Beach and was placed on multiple holds. I went to see a judge so that I could be released and not need to go directly into another program. I needed to figure it out on my own.

I decided to lock myself away, detaching from all family and friends. I had so much knowledge, there were things from each theory that worked, they weren't enough on their own. I looked for something that balanced the characteristics that I wanted for myself that also had measurement and reinforcement as main components.

When I couldn't find a system that worked, I created The Joy Codex and rigorously tested on myself, adjusting as I went in order to increase joy. I had to understand what it took to be a joyful person.

I shared my system with friends and family and spent time with them to teach them how to increase joy and sustain that joy, with successful results.

It is such a pleasure for me to have sustained joy and be free of alcohol and mind-altering substances. Something I thought would never be possible. Let me share with you how that was possible.

8 WHY THE JOY CODEX?

The Joy Codex is an action plan with the intelligent application of specific elements containing built in measurement and reinforcement in order to achieve a purpose; a joyful state.

I created The Joy Codex when all other therapies fell short and I continued to be sad, unhappy, and miserable. I was striving for **Secular Spiritual Homeostasis; an observance of a spiritual philosophy without adherence to a religion to achieve stable equilibrium maintained by physiological processes.**

In my darkest hours, I no longer wanted to end my life, although I had no reason to live. I pondered for many hours why I didn't want to live. My basic needs where being met, I should be happy. AWE! That was it, I wasn't happy.

I have always enjoyed feeling happy. More specifically, I enjoyed a joyful state.

What is different for me now, is that through The Joy Codex I've found a sweet spot or intrinsic motivation to remain clear in my head and body. I want to feel my emotions, understand them, I want to comprehend and remember behavior and how it leads to those emotions. I have achieved a joyful state.

Being joyful is a state of being rather than the feeling of joy during a joyous moment. Joyous moments come and go and are unpredictable; **a joyful state of being is the embodiment of those things that consistently increase joy on a regular basis.**

When I'm running on all cylinders, I can feel the joy in my heart and others may observe my joy which increases their joy.

Increasing joy is easier said than done though. I tried to be happy, I told myself to be happy, I told myself to get over it and be happy; on and on with little sustainable success. I created The Joy Codex when the theories and therapies I had been taught fell short of consistently increasing my joy. Knowing that I wanted to increase joy, I took the things that worked for me from each theory / therapy and created a cohesive methodology with the express intent of increasing my joy.

The beauty of The Joy Codex is that when I am implementing all the elements and actions earnestly and consistently, I increase joy for myself and others. The knock-on effects from The Joy Codex include a positive impact on my personal and professional relationships, a consistent joyful increase in my mood, and a positive change in my way of interacting with self and others.

It has taken me many years to gain the knowledge used to create The Joy Codex. It took another year to define the methodology and create the documents to support The Joy Codex (TJC).

Here are the important theories and therapies that have had an impact on how and why I created The Joy Codex.

Cognitive Behavioral Therapy (CBT) focuses on challenging and changing unhelpful cognitive distortions, your thoughts, beliefs, and attitudes, behaviors, improving emotional regulation, and the development of personal coping strategies that mitigate current problems. The cognitive model "hypothesizes that people's emotions and behaviors are influenced by their perceptions of events. It is not a situation in and of itself that determines what people feel but rather the way in which they construe a situation" (Beck, 1964).

Dialectical Behavioral Therapy (DBT) is comprised of four main components; mindfulness, distress tolerance, emotion regulation, and interpersonal effectiveness.

Mindfulness emphasizes improving an individual's ability to accept and be present in the current moment. Distress tolerance emphasizes increasing a person's tolerance of negative emotion, not trying to escape from that negative emotion. Emotion regulation emphasizes strategies to manage and change intense emotions that are causing issues. Interpersonal effectiveness emphasizes communication techniques that increase assertiveness, maintains self-respect, and strengthens relationships.

Performance Management "In simplest terms, it's a way of getting people to do what you want them to do and to like doing it. Performance Management is a scientifically based, data-oriented management system. It consists of three primary elements-measurement, feedback and positive reinforcement. Although each of these three elements can exist alone, all three must be present before you have true Performance Management. And they must be implemented systematically and in sequence." (Daniels, 2000)

Attachment Theory, "attachment is a deep and enduring emotional bond that connects one person to another across time and space." (Ainsworth, 1973; Bowlby, 1969)

Six Sigma has five main elements, define (D), measure (M), Analyze (A), Improve(I), and Control (C). Define the problem. Measure the problem. Analyze the cause of the problem. Improve, implement and verify the solution. Control and maintain the solution. DMAIC.

I have used the things that worked best for me in each of these therapies/theories, and combined them together in a cohesive methodology, The Joy Codex.

When I spent the week at Aubrey Daniels International (ADI) getting my certificate in performance management, Aubrey Daniels taught me the ABC's of behavior. A is the antecedent, what prompts or causes the behavior to occur. B is the behavior, the action. C is the consequence, what happens after the behavior.

These are important to know and understand in order to understand why people behave the way they do, the phone range (antecedent), I answered the phone (behavior), and I was delighted to be speaking with my agent (consequence).

The extra layer is the consequence, consequences can be positive or negative (P/N), immediate or future (I/F), known or unknown (K/U).

In my opinion the best is a PIC, positive, immediate, consequence. As an example, a PFU, positive, future, unknow is an example for smoking. I enjoy the cigarette right now, the consequence is off in the future and I may or may not get lung cancer, unknown.

The smoker knows that the outcome is going to most likely be negative, however, not certain, and the consequence is possible, but so far in the future that the consequence loses its impact. The most powerful consequences occur immediately after the behavior occurs.

In Aubrey Daniels book *I Saw What You Did & I Know Who You Are*, I learned that we spent more time on the outliers, usually putting our energy in the bottom 10%, managing by NIC, negative immediate consequence or penalty.

Aubrey Daniels says that "d*iscretionary effort is the level of effort people could give if they wanted to, but above and beyond the minimum required.*" In order to get discretionary effort, you must positively reinforce the behavior that leads to the requirement, a PIC, positive, immediate, consequence. **Increase their behavior by positive reinforcement and they will exceed your expectations.**

I created The Joy Codex SOaR worksheet (you will use this in later chapters) so that you will self-reinforce, I want you to soar with this schedule of reinforcement.

You will automatically be reinforced by some of your behavior, some of the consequences are immediate and some make themselves known at a later time.

Having a long talk with your child about speaking to others with compassion and integrity may appear to go unheard, nevertheless, you may see changes the following week. During the week after the discussion, you saw your child exhibiting the new behavior and gave them specific praise about their behavior, increasing the likelihood that they would continue to increase the wanted behavior.

This will increase your joy, seeing the new behavior, increasing your behavior to spend the time to discuss those tough subjects and provide reinforcement. As Aubrey Daniels stated "See It, Say It."

With Six Sigma, I get concrete data on any processes and can make changes that are measurable with the intention of improving the process. I also get to ask why 5 times in my search for the root cause of an issue. When developing The Joy Codex, I applied DMAIC consistently to achieve my purpose of increasing joy.

9 THE JOY CODEX TYPES OF PEOPLE

There are three types of people within The Joy Codex methodology; joyful, neutral, and unhappy.

I don't purport to be joyous twenty-four hours a day, and yet I consider myself a joyful person. I have ups and downs just like you, I don't always sleep well, I have stress, anxiety, disappointment, and loss.

The difference may reside in that fact that I choose to be keenly aware of these things. It is during these times that The Joy Codex is the first thing I reference so that I'm cognitive of my knowledge. I use those skills to think differently about my situation in a meaningful and positive way that creates positive change.

Awareness of my current state was important for me to make the choice to invest in the time required to learn and develop the skills necessary to increase joy.

Also, there's a myth in the world that if you were raised in an upwardly mobile family, what I often hear described as "a good family," that you had a well-rounded, safe, nurturing, stable, and loving environment to develop.

That absolutely isn't the truth. I'm a perfect example. From the outside you would see a "good family" that was full of dysfunction.

On the surface there was always an assumption that we were a good family and had a rather pleasant upbringing. From age one to seven my mother was receiving services from the county, bad things happened. My life from seven to fourteen was perceived as many to be well rounded and middle class, bad things happened.

As adults, sharing stories with my cousins convinced me that it didn't matter what kind of family you came from, as they had also been impacted by their caregivers. If you had caregivers that neglected (emotionally and/or physically), abused or were otherwise self-absorbed that there would be an increased likelihood you would have challenges in life.

Bad things happen to everyone, that is life. It's what we do with those negative events that determines the long-term outlook for a joyful life.

Traumatic events impact our lives differently, one event might be more than a person can handle and have zero impact on another. We can't know exactly how another person thinks or feels, we can have empathy or sympathy though.

Unhappy People

Unhappy people generally don't know that there is anything else, therefore they don't know they need help. Their unhappiness isn't due to socioeconomic status, it has more to do with the nurturing environment from their care givers.

A nurturing environment allows children to explore the world in an environment of emotional and physical safety and security.

In adulthood, many of the people that I meet in this category blame others for their suffering, feel that they are the victim and tend to have a negative outlook and approach to life. These people filter life through this lens.

I also often see narcissistic behaviors. It is interesting for me to have friends and family that fit within this category, many of their adult children now behave in the same way, negative and self-defeating comments towards self and others; and an overall defensiveness with a critical personality. This is a great time to take the steps necessary to achieve a joyful life and skip the next group, the neutral state of being.

Neutral People

Neutral people have been exposed to a life with a secure, happy, and well-rounded childhood, however they may have also been exposed to neglect (emotional and/or physical) and abuse from a self-absorbed caregiver in their life.

Neutral individuals generally blame others for their problems, feeling like they are the victim, and often they feel that the world is against them. My father called it the defeatist attitude.

They do have those wonderful moments; they know what it feels like to experience joy from the heart. Often this group will tell you how happy and positive they are, while in the same sentence make excuses for their behavior. **These people often bookend positive statements with negative ones, they have an overall pattern of negativity for self and others**.

I also see elements of narcissism within this group, but more often I see apathy. **These people still find comfort in their unhappiness, their needs are being met to some degree and they don't have all the skills and are too invested in their current life schema**.

Unless this group decides to get help, they tend to be the ones that will verbalize they don't need help but are clearly in need.

Many in this group also expresses negative self-defeating comments towards self and others, have an overall defensiveness, are judgmental, and have a critical personality. Those behaviors come and go dependent upon their needs being met. They are generally congenial when their needs are being met and appear to be well-rounded individuals. Watch out when those needs aren't being met though. There are many starts and stops in their search for well-being.

This is the time to make the jump to joy! This is the hardest group to change, this is where I was before I created The Joy Codex (TJC).

Joyful People

Joyful people look for solutions, are curious and even if they don't know the answer they continue to strive for improvement. Joyful people know that to achieve success, they must push forward with more dedication after each misstep.

Joyful people exert effort to determine what works rather than what doesn't, being cognitively aware of their actions and the outcome. They take the steps that lead to more joy, are engaged and active in gathering and using the skills necessary for a better life. Joyful people consistently exercise their new skills with the intention of strengthening and reinforcing the behaviors that lead to improvement.

Joyful people aren't in a state of eternal bliss, they can be negative, sad, moody, or irritable. We have all experienced the broad range of emotions in life. It is what you do today that makes the difference.

When I'm feeling irritable and must interact with others, I consciously slow down, listen, think, and start applying The Joy Codex. I choose to respond with compassion, integrity, responsibility, and clarity, those are the things that lead to a joyful emotional state.

Simply put, unhappy people don't know any better. Neutral people know better and have chosen to continue their pain and suffering, for whatever reason. Joyful people know there is more to life than misery and suffering and have made the conscious decision to acquire the tools and skills that increase joy.

There is a study that says 50% of happiness is determined by your genes, this is on a continuum, so it could be 40% or 60%. 10% of happiness is determined by your circumstances, the job you have, the car you drive, the house you may or may not own, shopping, your circle of friends. The things that almost all our society is focusing on, only give them a 10% boost in happiness. Sad. 40% of happiness is determined by your actions, your attitude, and your choices, making thoughtful decisions that lead to more happiness. The people that focus on the 40% live happier more well-rounded lives. These are the people that you want to be around. Focus on the 40% not the 10%, it's a better investment. That is what The Joy Codex is all about.

10 BARRIERS TO SUCCESS

Before we dive-in to The Joy Codex Method, I want to point out some barriers to success. If you have additional barriers to success, please identify them, place them aside, and review them once you have completed The Joy Codex in total (which includes the worksheets too).

Many of the barriers I was encountering were reduced, they were no longer insurmountable when I completed The Joy Codex.

I bring to your attention the two barriers that need be addressed up front, alcohol/substance use and apathy.

I used alcohol and mind-altering substances to decrease those feelings I didn't like. That didn't last forever however, alcohol and drugs lead to a significant increase in depression, anxiety, and a complete inability to formulate a plan to improve the situation.

Alcohol and drug consumption affect emotional regulation and response along with cognitive abilities like attention and memory **even when alcohol is no longer detectable.**

Even if a person doesn't abuse alcohol regularly or drink seven days a week, they will be impacted. I spoke with a medical professional familiar with the effects of alcohol, both emotionally and physically, he explained to me that it takes three to five days after drinking for the body to recover and the head to be clearer, to have normal cognition and emotional regulation.

That means if I get hammered over the weekend, I won't have clarity of thought, healthy emotional response and regulation, or normal cognitive ability until the following weekend. That certainly doesn't align with my integrity, as I'm not producing my best work.

While implementing The Joy Codex, reduction or abstinence of mind-altering substances and alcohol is my best advice. **Having a clear head to learn, comprehend, implement, and reinforce will garner the best results.** However as always, see a medical doctor before stopping any mind-altering substance, which includes alcohol.

Another barrier to success is apathy, which means a lack of feeling or emotion, a lack of interest or concern. Apathetic people are rather detached from their feelings and emotions as it relates to self and others.

These individuals have become indifferent and lack the motivation to decrease their pain and suffering. **Apathetic individuals have falsely concluded that the effort to live a more joyful life is greater than the reward**. They will remain unhappy and neutral by not taking the steps required to increase joy on a fundamental level.

Cognitive distortions are also a major barrier to success. "Cognitive distortions are thoughts that cause individuals to perceive reality inaccurately. According to the cognitive model of Beck, a negative outlook on reality, sometimes called *negative schemas* (or *schemata*), is a factor in symptoms of emotional dysfunction and poorer subjective well-being. **Specifically, negative thinking patterns cause negative emotions. During difficult circumstances, these distorted thoughts can contribute to an overall negative outlook on the world and a depressive or anxious mental state.**" (Wikipedia)

11 WHAT IS JOY?

Do you know what joy feels like? **I'm not talking about being happy, I'm talking about being in a joyful state.** Happy is defined as enjoying or characterized by well-being and contentment, having or marked by an atmosphere of good fellowship.

Joy is the emotion evoked by well-being, success, or good fortune or by the prospect of possessing what one desires, the expression or exhibition of such emotion, a state of happiness or felicity, a source or cause of delight.

Joyful is happiness with intelligent intention, with an understanding of the steps to success, and the determination to act. To achieve a joyful state, to increase a joyful state, and to sustain a joyful state requires the knowledge and tools necessary to succeed.

I often hear people say they are happy, and they get incensed when anyone attempts to help them achieve or increase joy. This is not a joyful person. **Defensiveness is the antitheses of a joyful state.** Being happy isn't a competition it's a way of living.

These people will tell you they are happy. However, when they communicate, they communicate with negativity. They will say "I'm only bitching," or "I'm only getting it off my chest."

Bitching or complaining, is a behavior that stems from negative thoughts that led to negative emotions about self and others; and isn't solution oriented.

Bitching and complaining is an attempt by the individual to divert attention from their own misery and suffering, that they themselves have chosen. When they bitch and complain, it is with negative intent and done out of resentment for others.

When you think negatively about yourself and others, you aren't in a joyful state. These thoughts are usually a cognitive distortion. When you speak to yourself and others with resentment, disdain, contempt, rudeness, anger, hatred, or apathy you aren't in a joyful state. When you drink alcohol every day or take mind-altering substances you aren't in a joyful state.

I'm able to quickly identify a person that isn't in a joyful state based on their behavior. Acting happy and saying nice things to other people doesn't make a joyful person. Being successful at the transactional things in life brings some happiness and a sense of accomplishment. It isn't enough to increase joy, joyful is a state a being not a transaction.

The way you communicate represents your state of being; in order to speak it, you must think it, which leads to feeling it and then behaving in that manner.

Remember there are 3 types of people, unhappy, neutral and joyful. Go back and reread that section on the three types of people if you are unsure.

I want to be clear; I want you to increase your joyful moments, this is going to take commitment, honesty, and action on your part. The results will speak for themselves based on your behavior.

12 WHAT IS THE JOY CODEX?

The Joy Codex is a rigorous set of values and principles I've developed, shared, and employed over my lifetime, with the express goal of achieving or increasing Joy.

There are five elements to The Joy Codex Methodology, the foundation being compassion, and then integrity, responsibility, clarity and joy. These concepts are applied to self and others in The Joy Codex.

The Joy Codex Pyramid

JOY

CLARITY

RESPONSIBILITY

INTEGRITY

COMPASSION

Codex Capstone Media L.L.C. ©   HWFAL002 L1

The levels of the pyramid are called elements when paired with action, and they represent specific characteristics. The elements include characteristics that start at the bottom with compassion and end at the capstone with joy. The characteristics where carefully chosen. Through trial and error, I selected the elements that most successfully increased my joy, in level of the impact they had on joy.

A clear understanding of the characteristics increases the likelihood for success in increasing joy, we will review each element in the next chapter. The elements build one upon another, don't skip any of the elements and follow the order I've prescribed.

Again, the elements of The Joy Codex build upon each other. The characteristics within each element were selected for their importance in building and sustaining a joyful life. The order is very important, compassion is the foundation of The Joy Codex, which leads to integrity, responsibility, clarity, and finally joy.

13 THE JOY CODEX METHODOLOGY

The Joy Codex Method

Choose	JOY
Operate W/	CLARITY
Demonstrate	RESPONSIBILITY
Elevate	INTEGRITY
eXemplify	COMPASSION

Codex Capstone Media L.L.C. ®

The Joy Codex Method (TJC)

Each of the characteristics also has an action verb, without action these characteristics are just words. **Action is behavior, behavior is life, life is changeable. Intelligent action specific to my behavior allows me to choose the life I want.**

The next portion is the behavior component, the action. Each elemental property or characteristic has an action verb applied. They are exemplify, elevate, demonstrate, operate, and choose. Exemplify compassion, elevate integrity, demonstrate responsibility, operate with clarity, and choose joy.

eXemplify as an action word means to show or lead by example.

Elevate as an action word means to lift-up, raise in rank, to improve morally, culturally, and intellectually.

Demonstrate as an action word means to show clearly, to make clear by reasoning or evidence, and to show value.

Operate as an action word means to perform a function, to produce an appropriate effect, and to perform a series of functions.

Choose as an action word means to select after consideration, to decide, to plan, and to have a preference.

Behavior is often known by the phrases 'taking action, acting, actions, or an action." Behavior or action must be observed (seen or heard) and is repeatable.

Let's take a couple of minutes to understand why The Joy Codex Method adds action to each characteristic.

The human brain evolved with the intent of our survival, allowing us to solve complex issues during our evolution. The key here is action, the brain had to develop in an environment with absolute uncertainty, little or no shelter, scarce food and water; and most importantly, the nomadic lifestyle.

We evolved to be hypervigilant in order to survive, alert for any threat, ready in a millisecond to react to a pouncing lion.

The brain was always alert, scanning the horizon for enemies, foraging for food and water, listening for sounds of impending danger, a cacophony of action for the sole purpose of survival. The brain is never idle.

Fast forward to modern man and our brains still function much like they did millions of years ago from a survival standpoint. *We survive with action, and action is something done to accomplish a purpose.*

The brain has plasticity and is changeable through specific behavior. That behavior when applied and reinforced strengthens the neural pathways that connect our brains.

A neural circuit is a population of neurons interconnected by synapses to carry out a specific function when activated. Neural circuits interconnect to one another to form large scale brain networks. (wikipedia.com)

When a new behavior is initiated, those neural circuits are activated and the paths (interconnection) between those circuits strengthen. Until the new neural pathway is strengthened, our brains will automatically select the strongest available pathway, the undesired old one.

With awareness and reinforcement, the new desired pathway will be reinforced becoming strong and prevalent, the old pathway will become less pronounced.

Here is an example, today when confronted with a rude person I automatically think negative thoughts about that person. This is an unwanted behavior; however, it is the most used neural path for this situation at this moment. This pathway is like the I-5, I-95, I-80, or I-10. These are major thoroughfares that carry a great deal of traffic and the most convenient and quickest way to get from point A to point B, traffic permitting.

Initiating new behavior and strengthening a neural pathway takes repetition and continued use.

When the wanted behavior is initiated it is akin to travelling on a dirt road. The neural pathway in the brain is not used very often and therefore a dirt road.

As the desired behavior is reinforced, and continues, that dirt road gets upgraded over time, it becomes a paved road, then it becomes a boulevard, with continued use it becomes an expressway and finally an interstate highway like the I-5.

The unwanted behavior will decrease due to the downgrade of the neural pathway associated with the unwanted behavior. The new behavior has been reinforced; the new upgraded brain pathway will become the path of choice.

The methodology applied in TJC is very deliberate, the base is the most important in order to achieve the apex or capstone. The characteristics build one upon another and they are in order of importance to achieve the capstone of joy. We will move up the elements, and apply what we've learned from the previous elements, and begin to have a positive impact on wellbeing.

The action word in front of each characteristic defines the behavior employed to achieve the characteristic. Notice that the Action column spells CODEX from top to bottom. **Without the action, which is the repeatable behavior, the characteristics are just words that we all embody to some degree, without intelligent application.**

Together, we will apply this technique, and don't worry, you don't need to try to remember every detail as you move forward. As your competence in the technique becomes more concrete you will automatically start to recall and employee the characteristics that bring joy and self-realization. You will ultimately achieve unconscious competence!

Self / Others

Everything I do to self; I do to others. Everything I do to others; I do to self. They are intimately connected. Actions (behavior) for and about self, have an impact on interactions with others. Behavior (actions) for and about another, impacts self.

Others, External Life

Wheel of Life

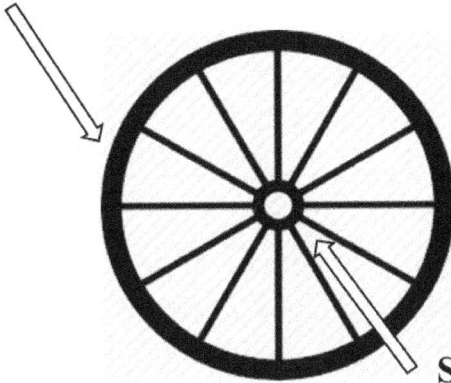

Self, Internal Life

BWWFAL005.4 www.thejoycodex.com   Codex Capstone Media L.L.C. ©

The outer ring of this wheel represents Others and also the persona you share with the world. The inner ring represents Self and your internal life.

The spokes represent your life experiences. The outer ring and inner ring are connected through the spokes. As you have new experiences throughout your life that are meaningful and important you add new spokes to your wheel of life.

When I learn a new life skill, I make a conscious decision to identify that spoke, what it means, how it is connected to the inner (Self) and outer (Others) rings, and where in the wheel it is located. This allows me to comprehend the new skill and utilize it to achieve a positive outcome.

Next we will explore each of the elements that make-up The Joy Codex.

14 EXEMPLIFY COMPASSION

What is compassion? Compassion is a sympathetic or empathetic consciousness of other's or self's' distress, together with a desire to mitigate or alleviate it.

Exemplify as an action word means to show or lead by example. Exemplifying compassion is showing positive feelings and emotions for self and others, leading by example. When I exemplify compassion for self and others; I feel.

eXemplify COMPASSION

eXemplify Compassion is the foundation and first key to unlocking The Joy Codex. Compassion makes us human; compassion allows us to feel empathy or sympathy for another's or our own suffering with a desire to alleviate that pain and suffering.

Psychologist Paul Eckman identified six basic emotions that he determined are universally experienced in all human cultures. The emotions he identified are happiness, sadness, disgust, fear, surprise, and anger. At a minimum, you should be familiar with these emotions.

As there are a broad range of emotions, compassion is detrimental to success. We humans can emulate and feel the emotions of others, this includes sadness, joy, fear, disgust, contempt, and love; to name a few.

Compassion for self and others is fundamental to succeeding in your desire to increase joy. The elements of The Joy Codex build one upon the other with compassion being the most intensive.

The action word for this element is exemplify. Remember that action is something done to accomplish a purpose. **There must be intelligent action in order to facilitate change.** Without the action, compassion is a nice word and concept. When I exemplify compassion for self and others, I feel.

The benefits of compassion have been studied extensively, the benefits are both physical and emotional. Compassion impacts the body physically, heart rate, blood pressure, breathing rate, immune system, diet, and sleep cycles are all examples. Compassion can also regulate emotion. Compassionate people reduce their anxiety and depression, while increasing feelings of joy and connection. **Compassion enables us to understand ourselves and others as we engage in behavior with the intent of relieving suffering.**

In my daily interactions with people, I've noticed that most would describe themselves as compassionate people, feeling sympathetic to another's pain and suffering. This is where compassion stops for most people. **Compassion also includes the desire to mitigate or alleviate pain and suffering for self.** It is often difficult for people to extend any compassion for their own pain and suffering. Having compassion for self, is absolutely critical to having compassion for others.

I had a difficult time extending compassion to myself until I could truly express it for others. In fact, I was unable to extend compassion to self until I had an experience dealing with another person. This person consistently interrupted, was rude, made inappropriate comments, and could only hear their own voice.

In my dealings with this person, I learned that this person had a traumatic brain injury, and by no fault of their own, their behavior had changed. I was disappointed that I had made a judgment about this person without knowing more about them. I felt compassion for this person so deeply that I learned to feel compassion for myself. I discovered what compassion meant and felt like, it was like a wave washed over me.

There is a great deal to compassion as is relates to oneself or to another. Compassionate communication with self and others is vital to understanding this element. Communication with others is conveyed with compassion. That means speaking to another without resentment, contempt, rudeness, anger, divisiveness or defensiveness. Speaking to another with compassion encompasses intention. Listening with the same intention, responding with patience, compassion, and kindness.

Communication with self is just as important. Increase positive internal dialogue. Thoughts lead to emotions and emotions lead to behavior. If you put poor quality gasoline (negative inner self- talk) in your vehicle, it won't operate (behavior) as expected. **Expressions of compassion for self will have the greatest impact on thoughts, emotions, and the resulting behaviors. Put simply, if you are having unsatisfactory emotions, your thoughts are the culprit.**

When I started expressing compassion for self via positive internal dialogue, I immediately noticed a change in my behavior towards self and others. **Positive internal dialogue had a direct impact on my behavior towards others**. It's difficult to feel compassion for another when I'm unable to extend compassion to myself.

Interestingly, now when I hear another communicating about self in a negative manner, it immediately jumps out to me, I hear the self-defeating comments every time. I never noticed the negative verbalizations in the past, compassion for self and others created that awareness.

Minding the gap will also increase compassion. This is an important skill to learn. Minding the gap, the amount of time after thought but before a reaction or response. Minding the gap is the difference between reacting to a situation versus responding to a situation. I do use this skill often.

I was recently interacting with an unhappy, negative, hostile, and rude individual. I had to consciously mind the gap, in fact **I had to extend that gap**. My initial thought was they were verbally attacking me, I wanted to go on the attack. When I took that extra second to apply compassion to self and others, I was able to respond in a way that increased my joy.

It's important to understand that we as individuals may express compassion, however, we are unable to view the world exactly as another does. **Each person comes with years of unique experiences. Everyone has different education, socioeconomic, employment, and religious backgrounds that are specific to that individual.** We are unable to view the world through the exact same filter as another. Therefore, compassion with others is critical, even when they are unpleasant.

My intention is to walk away from every interaction knowing I did everything to increase joy for myself and others. That includes communicating with compassion even when it's difficult.

There are many ways to exemplify compassion for self and others, smile at strangers, get the door for someone, spend more time with a sick relative, volunteer, read The Joy Codex, extend an olive branch, help a coworker, or increase positive internal dialogue. Meditation is also an excellent way to increase compassion, as meditation activates regions of the brain that regulate emotion.

Having an awareness of what compassion is and how it feels when applied to self and others is also a way to exemplify compassion. Having an awareness of compassion for self and others means living in the present, extending compassion to self and others today.

Live for today and not the past or future. The past is unchangeable, and the future is unknowable. This doesn't mean that you should abandon your future plans. Planning is wise.

Once I understood what compassion for self and others meant, I had to remove all the barriers that prevented me from exemplifying compassion. Knowing my physical and emotional rhythms and cycles also increased my ability to exemplify compassion for self and others.

If I am feeling down, there is a good chance that my interactions with others may reflect my emotions. I am aware that my communications need extra care.

I specifically added reinforcement and measurement to the Joy Codex to increase the desired behavior. The reinforcement causes an increase in behavior and the measurement scores the current state. There is still a need for you to be invested in the process and have a deep commitment to a more joyful and complete life.

People that aren't compassionate or don't truly know what it means to be compassionate exhibit a lack of understanding and concern for self and others.

A lack of compassion for self and others can be easily identified, these people often consistently exhibit self-centered, arrogant, callous, cold, confrontational, cruel, cynical, defensive, distant, hostile, impatient, impolite, inconsiderate, indiscreet, inflexible, intolerant, irresponsible, jealous, moody, narrow-minded, nasty, overcritical, pessimistic, possessive, quick-tempered, resentful, rude, thoughtless, and unreliable behavior. I put every adjective I could think of here because knowing these behaviors and identifying them when observed is knowing how to change them.

When these behaviors are exhibited regularly and not a onetime action, you have encountered an unhappy or neutral person.

Having compassion doesn't mean that I'm a doormat, it doesn't mean that I allow others to take advantage of me or walk all over me. Having compassion, I understand that I don't and can't know **exactly** what another person is thinking or feeling. I'm not a mind reader or a fortune teller. When someone shares a story with me, I can feel sympathy or empathy, however I can't know all their life experiences and I can't see the world through the exact same filter or lens.

By considering and applying compassion to self and others I am able to set personal and professional boundaries. Boundaries are important, some boundaries are set in stone, immoveable, while other boundaries are more fluid and they change as you change.

Define your limits, when you are feeling anxious and uncomfortable seeing or hearing another's behavior, a boundary most likely needs to be set.

If a person is nasty to others around me and I feel anxious and uncomfortable, I set a boundary that I will only speak to that person directly and limit my interactions.

It's important to know what makes you feel uncomfortable when setting boundaries. Setting boundaries out of resentment may achieve the desired behavior from the other party, it won't achieve the emotion you are intending to increase, joy.

Set boundaries for the correct reasons and communicate them in advance, not after the boundary has been crossed.

Be clear cognitively and emotionally about any boundary you have in place, know the specifics so that you know when a boundary is being crossed.

Don't confuse boundaries with passive-aggressive behavior, there is real concern when setting boundaries. Setting boundaries as a tit-for-tat approach isn't healthy for you in the long run.

When you do set a boundary, it is best to share that boundary with others when that line is crossed. Remember that just as we aren't mind readers, others aren't either. If the people in your life aren't accustomed to you setting boundaries, be prepared for some pushback.

They were getting their needs met on some level while you weren't, this causes resentment. Now that you have a boundary in place, they will be uncomfortable initially. **Remember, you don't have to be a people pleaser all the time especially when you are feeling anxious and uncomfortable.**

In Catherine Beard's book *How to Set Healthy Boundaries,* there are seven things you can do to set healthy boundaries. "Get clear on your priorities, communicate what you will and will not tolerate, listen to your gut instinct, think about the impact of your actions, do things because they make you happy, offer an alternative, and be direct and firm with your answer."

Boundaries are important when initiating a plan of action that includes The Joy Codex and the elements of The Joy Codex.

Barriers to Success

Specifically, to the element of compassion, apathy is a major barrier to success. Apathy which means a lack of feeling or emotion, a lack of interest or concern. Apathetic people are rather detached from their feelings and emotions as it relates to self and others, this hinders compassion. Awareness of your feelings for self and others at all times is critical to improving those feelings.

Excessive or prolonged use of alcohol and/or mind-altering substances is also one of those barriers to a comprehensive strategy of compassion for self and others. As I developed The Joy Codex this became very evident. I initially drank to escape pain and suffering, both emotional and physical. I also liked to drink alcohol when I went out, I thought it was the libation that lubricated conversation. Alcohol and mind-altering substances prohibit you from regulating your emotions, which means you are unable to regulate your thoughts.

Final Thoughts

When I exemplify compassion, I feel. Applying compassion to self and others is a learned behavior and available to everyone. Compassion is foundational to The Joy Codex, thoughts influence emotions, having thoughts of compassion will influence your feelings of compassion.

Knowing that others come with their own life experiences and see the world through a different filter than you will help you increase your compassion.

In order to move to the next element of integrity, you must understand and have compassion for self and others. If you're unable to be cognitively compassionate, you'll be unable to feel compassion, which makes it difficult to be integrous.

Think about compassion in the things you say and do and be aware of the moments you feel compassion. Knowing when you are feeling compassion and how that feeling came about will help you connect thoughts to emotions and behavior.

Worksheets

All forms are online at www.thejoycodex.com/forms. The worksheets are for you, this is your information, how you feel, and what you think. There aren't any right or wrong answers, the rank is there to give you a consistent measurement of where you are for that category at that moment allowing you to benchmark and improve.

I placed my worksheets/documents in a three-ring binder for organization and ease of review to determine my success.

Complete honesty when answering the worksheets exemplifies compassion. A score achieved through dishonesty only serves to exacerbate your misery, the score isn't a competition. When you know what your score is from day to day, you have the ability to make changes that will increase your score the following day.

Now that you've completed the chapter on compassion, it's time to put what you've learned into action! This is the fun part! Know that you are making intelligent choices combined with intention and action.

In order to implement The Joy Codex Methodology, you will need to utilize the following forms. Continuation of the new behavior requires reinforcement; the forms below will provide everything you need. Complete each of the worksheets for the duration listed below using the instructions provided.

Print enough copies of each worksheet based on the instructions below. For best results follow the directions exactly. I recommend that you place worksheets in a three-ring binder for organization and ease for reviewing your progress and success.

At the end of the book, there are additional worksheets that may be of value to you today. Please review these worksheets and determine if they are applicable for that moment. The worksheets are the "SOaR Monthly," "What Element Could I Have Applied," "Change My Thoughts, Emotions, Behaviors" "Thoughts, Emotions, Behaviors," and "The Behavior I want, via, Thought and Emotion."

The Joy Codex Survey Compassion (Days 1 and Day 7) 2 copies.

THE JOY CODEX SURVEY COMPASSION

Name: _____ Date: _____ TJC Rank: _____

	Pick one answer per question that best describes your current feelings about compassion.	ANSWER							Score	Weight	Total
1	Do you know what compassion for Self feels like?	Y	S	N	NS					3	
2	How often do you feel compassion for Self?**	D	W	M	Q	A	N	NS		3	
3	Are you aware of those moments of compassion for Self?	Y	S	N	NS					2	
4	Are you aware of the things you do that increase compassion for Self?	Y	S	N	NS					2	
5	Do you exemplify compassion for Self?	Y	S	N	NS					3	
6	Do you create situations with compassion for Self in mind?	Y	S	N	NS					3	
7	Do you feel compassion for Others?	Y	S	N	NS					4	
8	Do you create situations that increase compassion for Others?	Y	S	N	NS					4	
9	Do you start each day with the intention to increase compassion for Self and Others?	Y	S	N	NS					5	
10	Do you want more compassion in your life for Self and Others?	Y	S	N	NS					4	
11	Do you have the skill and tools to increase compassion in your life?	Y	S	N	NS					5	
12	Are you willing to dedicate your time and energy to increasing your Compassion?	Y	S	N	NS					5	

Sum Total:

KEY Y=YES, S=SOMETIMES, N=NEVER, NS=NOT SURE — Sum Total /10:

**DAILY/WEEKLY/MONTHLY/QUARTERLY/ANNUALLY/NEVER /NOT SURE (pick one) — New Total*2:

Round Totals Up or Down to Nearest Decimal

Key Score		Measurement Rules	Rankings
Y	6		49-52 Joyful +
N	1	In order to get the TJC Rank, multiply the Score column by the Weight column for each question.	44-48 Joyful
SOMETIMES	3	Enter that number in the Total column. Add the Total column and enter that number in to the Sum Total field.	39-43 Joyful -
NOT SURE	2	Divide the number in the Sum Total field by 10 and rounding up or down to the nearest decimal. Enter that	33-38 Neutral +
DAILY	6	number in the Sum Total / 10 field. Multiply the Sum Total / 10 field by 2, rounding up or down to nearest decimal.	27-32 Neutral
WEEKLY	5	Enter that number in the New Total*2 field. Compare that number to the Rankings and enter your ranking	16-26 Neutral -
MONTHLY	4	in the TJC Rank field at the top of the form. As an example, if I scored 39, I would write out Joyful-	≤ 15 Unhappy
QUARTERLY	3		
ANNUALLY	2		
NEVER	1		

BWWCN0015 — www.thejoycodex.com — Codex Capstone Media L.L.C.©

Take the Joy Codex Survey on days 1 and 7. You may take the survey all 7 days to get an extra little bit of boost as you start each day. The survey is a gage for you to understand your current feelings about compassion and will get you grounded in the new element you have just learned about. The measurement on the worksheet is a benchmark for you to increase your results based on your answers. You will know which areas to improve upon for the next day, you will be more focused.

The Joy Codex Elements In Action Compassion (Days 1-7) 1 copy used throughout the 7 days.

The Joy Codex Elements In Action		Compassion	
Exemplify Compassion		**Lack of Compassion**	
1	Demonstrating concern for the misery and suffering of Self and Others.	1	Demonstrating little or no concern for the misery and suffering of Self and Others.
2	Increased compassion when those that suffer receive relief.	2	Clear resentment when Others are receiving compassion.
3	Communicating with cognitive intention and compassion in mind.	3	Communicating with resentment, negativity, and selfishness.
4	Helping the needy/volunteering.	4	Disdain for the needy.
5	Desire to see Self and Others in a joyful state.	5	No concern for Self and Others emotional state.
6	Showing concern for Self and Others well-being.	6	Little or no concern for Self and Others well-being.
7	Acting with the intention of compassion.	7	Acting without concern for Others.
8		8	
9		9	
10		10	
11		11	
12		12	
13		13	
14		14	
15		15	
16		16	

Use the spaces provided to add the items you have identified that exemplify compassion and the items that don't. How do your thoughts influence your compassion with regard to self and others? How will you exemplify compassion and what is the opposite of your action item, how will you know when it isn't demonstrated?

BWWCN005.4   www.thejoycodex.com   Codex Capstone Media L.L.C.©

The Joy Codex Elements In Action worksheet challenges you to put your knowledge into action and to be cognitively aware when your actions are incongruent with The Joy Codex.

The Joy Codex Inventory Integrity (Days 1-7) 1 copy used throughout the 7 days.

The Joy Codex Inventory Compassion

List the things that exemplify compassion for Self and Others.

Self	Others
1	1
2	2
3	3
4	4
5	5
6	6
7	7
8	8
9	9
10	10
11	11
12	12
13	13
14	14
15	15
16	16
17	17
18	18
19	19
20	20

BWWCN0004.0   www.thejoycodex.com   Codex Capstone Media L.L.C.

The Joy Codex Inventory details the things you are doing to identify and increase the elemental behavior. During the 7 days, you will identify new items/people/places/things that demonstrate that element, add them to the inventory.

The Joy Codex Quick Start Compassion (Days 1-7, at the start of your day) 7 copies.

THE JOY CODEX QUICK START COMPASSION

Name: _____ Date: _____ TJC Rank: _____

	Pick one answer per question that best describes your action plan for success today.	ANSWER				Score	Weight	Total
1	I know what TJC compassion entails for Self and Others today.	Y	S	N	NS		5	
2	I will exemplify compassion for Self and Others today.	Y	S	N	NS		4	
3	I will have patience with Self and Others today.	Y	S	N	NS		3	
4	I will be kind to Self and Others today.	Y	S	N	NS		3	
5	I will think positively about Self and Others today.	Y	S	N	NS		3	
6	I will listen intently when interacting with Others today.	Y	S	N	NS		3	
7	I will respond to Others with compassion today.	Y	S	N	NS		4	
8	When I experience compassion for Self and Others today, I will be aware of that emotion.	Y	S	N	NS		4	
9	I will identify the interactions that increase my compassion for Self and Others today.	Y	S	N	NS		5	
10	I will complete the Quick Wrap Compassion worksheet today.	Y	S	N	NS		4	
11	I will complete the SOaR worksheet today.	Y	S	N	NS		5	

KEY Y=YES, S=SOMETIMES, N=NEVER, NS=NOT SURE

Sum Total: _____
Sum Total /10: _____
New Total*2: _____

Round Totals Up or Down to Nearest Decimal

Key Score		Measurement Rules	Rankings
Y	6	In order to get the TJC Rank, multiply the Score column by the Weight column for each question.	49-52 Joyful +
N	1	Enter that number in the Total column. Add the Total column and enter that number in to the Sum Total field.	44-48 Joyful
SOMETIMES	3	Divide the number in the Sum Total field by 10 and rounding up or down to the nearest decimal. Enter that	39-43 Joyful -
NOT SURE	2	number in the Sum Total / 10 field. Multiply the Sum Total / 10 field by 2, rounding up or down to nearest decimal	33-38 Neutral +
		Enter that number in the New Total*2 field. Compare that number to the Rankings and enter your ranking	27-32 Neutral
		in the TJC Rank field at the top of the form. As an example, if I scored 39, I would write out Joyful-	16-26 Neutral -
			≤ 15 Unhappy

BWWCN002.0 www.thejoycodex.com Codex Capstone Media L.L.C.©

The Joy Codex Quick Start worksheet is an antecedent, the worksheet will prompt you at the start of your day to focus on specific points within the worksheet based on the unique element you are working on. This will be completed at the start of each day. The Quick Start worksheet has specific "I" statements to prepare your brain for success that day. The measurement on the form is a benchmark for you to increase your results based on your answers. You will know which areas to improve upon for the next day, you will be more focused.

The Joy Codex Quick Wrap Compassion (Days 1-7 at the end of your day) 7 copies.

THE JOY CODEX QUICK WRAP COMPASSION

Name: _____ Date: _____ TJC Rank: _____

	Pick one answer per question that best describes your success for today.	ANSWER				Score	Weight	Total
1	Today I knew what TJC compassion was for Self and Others.	Y	S	N	NS		5	
2	Today I exemplifyed compassion for Self and Others.	Y	S	N	NS		4	
3	Today I had patience for Self and Others.	Y	S	N	NS		3	
4	Today I was kind to Self and Others.	Y	S	N	NS		3	
5	Today I thought positively about Self and Others.	Y	S	N	NS		3	
6	Today I listened intently when interacting with Others.	Y	S	N	NS		3	
7	Today I responded to Others with compassion.	Y	S	N	NS		4	
8	Today when I experienced compassion for Self and Others today, I was aware of that emotion.	Y	S	N	NS		4	
9	Today I identified the interactions that increased my compassion for Self and Others.	Y	S	N	NS		5	
10	Today I Completed the Quick Wrap Compassion.	Y	S	N	NS		4	
11	Today I completed the SOaR worksheet.	Y	S	N	NS		5	

KEY Y=YES, S=SOMETIMES, N=NEVER, NS=NOT SURE

Sum Total:
Sum Total /10:
New Total*2:
Round Totals Up or Down to Nearest Decimal

Key Score		Measurement Rules	Rankings
Y	6	In order to get the TJC Rank, multiply the Score column by the Weight column for each question.	49-52 Joyful +
N	1	Enter that number in the Total column. Add the Total column and enter that number in to the Sum Total field.	44-48 Joyful
SOMETIMES	3	Divide the number in the Sum Total field by 10 and rounding up or down to the nearest decimal. Enter that	39-43 Joyful -
NOT SURE	2	number in the Sum Total / 10 field. Multiply the Sum Total / 10 field by 2, rounding up or down to nearest decimal.	33-38 Neutral +
		Enter that number in the New Total*2 field. Compare that number to the Rankings and enter your ranking	27-32 Neutral
		in the TJC Rank field at the top of the form. As an example, if I scored 39, I would write out Joyful-	16-26 Neutral -
			≤ 15 Unhappy

BWWCN003.0   www.thejoycodex.com   Codex Capstone Media L.L.C.©

The Joy Codex Quick Wrap worksheet is a review of your day specific to the element you are implementing. The questions are designed to stimulate your thought process about your day specific to each question and your application of the component. There is an expectation that you will review your day mentally and answer the questions thoughtfully. The measurement on the worksheet is a benchmark for you to know where you stand that day and to improve your results based on your answers to the questions and your you rank. You will know which areas to improve upon for the next day, you will be more focused.

The Joy Codex SOaR Daily Log (Day 1-7 at the end of your day) 7 copies.

The Joy Codex SOaR Daily Log			
Date	Rank (circle one icon that represents your day)		Score

Today I had a ___ TJC RANK ___ day because ___ the reasons you ranked Unhappy or Neutral or Joyful

Tomorrow I will ___ detail the actions you will take to increase your success

TJC Rank			Name:
5 Unhappy	5	10	15	
10 Neutral		Key Score		Rank:
15 Joyful			

BWWBR001.0   www.thejoycodex.com   Codex Capstone Media L.L.C.

The Joy Codex SOaR Daily Log is a schedule of reinforcement. The form is very simple to use, there are three icons, ▢ ▢ ▰ you will select the one that best represents how your day went in relation to applying the new skills and tools you are learning. From left to right the icons represent a day that required charging as you were unable to implement the element as desired. The middle icon represents a day that didn't go 100% as planned. You started your day with the Quick Start worksheet, you were cognizant of the specific items within each element, however, you found yourself slipping back into old behavior. The icon on the right is the full charge battery, this is a great day. You were completely aware of the Quick Start items that day and knew when you implemented them. The worksheet also has two statements from you; what the specific reasons were for your ranking that day, and a statement about what you will do specifically the next day to improve and succeed. The measurement on the worksheet is a benchmark for you to increase your results based on your answers. You will know which areas to improve upon for the next day, you will be more focused.

15 ELEVATE INTEGRITY

What is integrity? Integrity is an adherence to a code especially moral or artistic values, an unimpaired condition, and the quality or state of being complete or undivided.

Elevate as an action word means to lift-up, raise in rank, to improve morally, culturally, and intellectually. Elevating integrity is knowing that you act ethically, morally, and with values every time. When I elevate integrity; I know.

Elevate Integrity is the second key to unlocking The Joy Codex and builds upon what was learned within the exemplify compassion element. Without integrity social bonds, morals, values, and ethical behavior begin to suffer and break down.

If compassion wasn't so critical to the foundation of TJC, I would have selected integrity as the foundation. They are very close though in importance. If I don't have integrity in dealing with others,

I lose all hope of building a relationship on trust and developing meaningful bonds. This applies to self too.

Without integrity for self, doubt creeps in, negative inner dialogue increases, and trust in societal ethics, mores, and norms begin to break down. Having trust in social mores and norms is important in building integrity societally, if others see me elevate integrity, that social trust grows, and others strive to elevate integrity by my example. My integrity for self has a direct impact on the integrity of others.

Physiologically, your thoughts cause the release of natural chemicals within your body, inducing emotion. Integrity requires positive thinking about self and others. As an example; when you see a loved one and you think and feel those emotions, your body is releasing oxytocin. Conversely, when most people see a snake, they think and feel fear, the body is releasing the hormone cortisol. We become what we think.

Making the choices that elevate cognitive integrity means that you are thinking in ways that are conducive to your well-being. You have a responsibility to think with integrity.

Do you know how to elevate integrity? **Elevating integrity requires an understanding of your values, beliefs, spirituality, and ethics; these are fundamental to who you are and what you represent**. Integrity requires action, without action integrity is greatly reduced or nonexistent.

Have you ever taken office supplies from work without permission? Do you think removing office supplies from the office without authorization is permissible? Exhibiting integrity always dictates not taking paperclips, copy paper, or pens and pencils from work. When I observe individuals that act with low integrity it becomes clear that the individual has suspended their integrity for the purpose of taking the office supplies that they don't own, they often feel that the supplies are "owed" to them.

Not running the freeway on-ramp red light is another one that I often see and have discussed with friends and family. If other people are going to run the light, why shouldn't they? This goes back to my argument that my actions have an impact on another's integrity, leading by example. **Suspending integrity to benefit one's self is a lack of moral character, ethics, and values.** Integrity is always applied to every situation.

Remember that your thoughts direct your emotions and those emotions direct your behavior. Integrity with your thoughts towards self and others directly influences how you feel about yourself and others, which translates into your behavior.

Because thoughts, positive versus negative, for self and others is so critical to your success I am going to discuss thoughts in each element, it's one of the common components of The Joy Codex, a part of each element.

I live in San Clemente, CA, and we've had an "invasion" of homeless that started an encampment on one of our main public beaches. Due to legal action, the encampment was moved to a public lot, that was fenced, until another solution could be found. The city can't legally arrest or otherwise evict the homeless. It isn't illegal to camp-out in public places if the city doesn't offer homeless shelter services. Incidentally, we will have homeless services shortly and then the homeless can be evicted from camping on public lands.

The outrage and hatred for these homeless isn't a secret, there are even Facebook pages dedicated to the hatred. Many of the citizens of this great city have such disdain for these homeless that their feelings and emotions have turned negative and now the behavior of these individuals demonstrates those feelings. The verbal hate speech and physical altercations have increased dramatically from the residents. There is a direct link between negative thoughts of others and negative behavior towards others.

I do believe there are some that have joined this encampment with nefarious purposes, as has been proven, that doesn't mean that all of the homeless in our city are bad people doing bad things, its asinine to think that.

What surprises me most about the homeless issue and integrity of thought for others, is that most of these people identify as religious god-fearing people. Disdain for the homeless is incongruent with religion.

When I think negative thoughts about another, however minor, my feelings about that person also turn negative. Once my emotions about that person become negative **my behavior towards them also becomes negative**. Those negative thoughts of others that turn into negative emotions about others also ricochet back to you and increase your negative feelings about self.

Negative thoughts for self will lead to negative thoughts for others. Negative thoughts for others will lead to negative thoughts for self. Those negative thoughts perpetuate those negative emotions and behaviors. When you elevate integrity for your thoughts about self and others, you increase positive emotion, behavior, and compassion for self and others. We want to increase joy, elevating integrity for self and others is prescribed.

I still have negative automatic thoughts and false beliefs that come to the surface of my conscious awareness, it is my responsibility to address those thoughts and beliefs in a positive compassionate way and with integrity. The automatic thoughts and beliefs; when negative, increase negative emotions. By addressing these thoughts with integrity and compassion, I now have automatic thoughts that are positive about self and others. The positive automatic thoughts are a beautiful consequence of The Joy Codex, my emotions and behavior automatically improved.

Do you hear others speak to people with the intent to cause pain, hurt, and suffering by use of inappropriate verbiage? **In order to behave in such a manner, the other person has consistently engaged in negative thoughts, leading to negative emotions directed at the person they are behaving negatively towards**. If you have friends, family, or roommates that fit into this category, be aware, in order to speak (behave) that way, they are thinking that way.

Cognitive integrity also includes how you speak to people, your communications are conveyed without the *intent* to harm, manipulate, disgrace, hurt or otherwise cause pain and suffering. I underline intent because your communications may cause another pain, though they weren't conveyed with the intent to cause pain or suffering.

When my communications leave me with good intent, I don't feel guilty later even when I must set boundaries or talk about painful or tough subjects. When dealing with others that communicate with contempt, disdain, scorn, or hurtful intent I employ compassion as I'm unable to view the world exactly as they view the world, through their personal filters, and I respond with integrity.

Minding the gap, that moment between a reaction or a response is also a component of integrity. The gap can be extended with practice. Rather than reacting with an emotional outburst you will later regret, take a moment, think and then **respond** with integrity.

I also set boundaries when interacting with others that don't employ integrity in their communications, and in some cases, ending those relationships, having compassion for myself.

Values, morals, ethics, and honesty are more than concepts to be used in communications, they require consistent and rigorous application to real life situations, they can't be fluid. You have integrity or you don't. **Applying integrity when it benefits you and not applying integrity when inconvenient doesn't elevate integrity.** An integrous person consistently applies integrity in all areas of their life.

Integrity and honesty go hand in hand. Being honest with yourself is important, and a requirement for integrity. Keeping commitments to self is just as important as keeping your commitments with others. Also, make commitments to self with compassion in mind.

I have a friend that consistently goes all out to lose weight, buys the right food, tosses everything else in the cupboard out and earnestly attempts to diet until self-doubt and negative inner dialogue gets the better of him. Comfort food here he comes!

This is the time to have compassion for him and hope that he is compassionate with himself. With integrity and compassion, I don't make promises to myself that I can't keep and if I do overshoot my ability to meet those obligations I reevaluate and implement change.

Integrity may be accomplished with or without supernatural guidance. Coming from an extremely religious family, I often hear that without religion there can't be integrity or hope in the world. I disagree, integrity is an intrinsic quality that includes our values, beliefs, morals, honesty, and spirituality (secular and religious). Non-religious people have integrity, experience joy, and are spiritual.

Even though I believe in a higher power, I don't need guidance from God in order to know that stealing isn't ethical or legal and goes against my spirituality and values. That is integrity.

There is a myth that goes something like this, if you aren't religious you can't be spiritual. That isn't factual.

Spirituality is defined as the quality or state of being spiritual. Spiritual is relating to, consisting of, or affecting the spirit. There are 14 definitions for the word spirit, here are the first 7. An animating or vital principle held to give life to physical organisms, a supernatural being or essence, an often malevolent being that is bodiless but can become visible, a malevolent being that enters and possesses a human being, temper or disposition of mind or outlook especially when vigorous, **the immaterial intelligent or sentient part of a person, the activating or essential principle influencing a person, an inclination, impulse, or tendency of a specified kind, a special attitude or frame of mind, the feeling, quality, or disposition characterizing something, and a lively or brisk quality in a person or a person's actions.**

I bolded the definitions for spirit that aren't expressly associated with a deity. An individual may associate these to a deity, that is a personal preference. For me, placing the responsibility of integrity in a deity's hands removes an individual's responsibility for acting with integrity.

Those that espouse integrity and don't act accordingly, pick and choose the values, morals, and ethics they want to exhibit and at what time, this is a concern and appropriate boundaries may need to be initiated. **Integrity is applied consistently, with or without the need for deital guidance**.

Mind the gap, before acting without thought or intelligence, decide how to respond to a communication, situation, task, person, and self, asking yourself "will this elevate integrity, does this action align with my values, ethics, morals, and spirituality." If the action isn't in alignment, consider another course of action.

Boundary setting within the context of integrity means knowing that in order to achieve success, setting boundaries is the correct action. They must be identified, set, and communicated.

I set boundaries when I am required to interact with deceitful, dishonest, unethical, resentful, sneaky, untrustworthy, inflexible, intolerant, tactless, unpredictable, impatient, unreliable, irresponsible, and selfish individuals. I'm actively moving away from these negative traits for self and others, increasing integrity in my life.

Remember that doing the right thing every time for self and others is the second characteristic because doing the right thing builds awareness, trust, respect, concern, compassion, and increases the bonds we have with others; increasing joy.

Barriers to Success

A barrier to success within the element of integrity is perfectionism. Are you a perfectionist? Does everything need to be 1000% all the time? This may come as a surprise, perfection is subjective.

Perfection is viewed through personal filters that have been developed over a lifetime. I can't know everything a person has gone through, so their version of perfection is different than everyone else that I encounter.

As an example, I'm hard on myself when it comes to anything artistic, I have this vision in my head that often doesn't materialize causing me frustration with myself.

I now believe that what I create is what was intended and knowing that I did my best means my artwork is just right at that moment. I enjoy my art now and engage in activities that include artistic expression.

My skillset isn't being an artist, I accept and have compassion for myself, I excel at language and science, that is my gig.

I'm not perfect, I'm "just right;" always doing my best in all things. What is perfect for me isn't for you. I always do the right thing, which includes putting my complete best effort forward for any task or interaction, professionally and personally.

Elevating integrity is doing the right thing all the time even when others aren't looking and no one knows, in other words no "atta boy" from others; only self. This includes following the laws of the land.

One of the definitions of integrity is "an unimpaired condition" which indicates that integrity includes not being cognitively challenged because of alcohol and substance abuse. This is especially important as you implement The Joy Codex.

Final Thoughts

When I elevate integrity, I know. Cognitive integrity is knowing that you behave ethically, morally, and with values every time. You know the difference and what it takes to be an integrous person. Rather than interpreting what others say, repeat back to them what you think they meant. This gives them the opportunity to more clearly explain themselves and you won't assume. Be integrous with your thought and your word. Remember that thoughts influence behavior.

Complete honesty when answering the worksheets elevates integrity. A score achieved through dishonesty only serves to exacerbate your misery, the score isn't a competition. When you know what your score is from day to day, you have the ability to make changes that will increase your score the following day.

Now that you've completed the chapter on integrity, it's time to put what learned into action! Again, this is the fun part! Know that you are making intelligent choices combined with intention and action to achieve a goal.

Worksheets

Applying integrity to self and others is a learned behavior and available to everyone. Let's get started, all forms are online at www.thejoycodex.com/forms

In order to implement The Joy Codex Methodology, you will need to utilize the following forms. Continuation of the new behavior requires reinforcement; the forms below will provide everything you need. Complete each of the worksheets for the duration listed below using the instructions provided.

Print enough copies of each worksheet based on the instructions below. For best results follow the directions exactly.

At the end of the book, there are additional worksheets that may be of value to you today. Please review these worksheets and determine if they are applicable for that moment. The worksheets are the "SOaR Monthly," "What Element Could I Have Applied," "Change My Thoughts, Emotions, Behaviors" "Thoughts, Emotions, Behaviors," and "The Behavior I want, via, Thought and Emotion."

The Joy Codex Survey Integrity (Days 1 and 7) 2 copies.

THE JOY CODEX SURVEY   INTEGRITY

Name: Date: TJC Rank:

	Pick one answer per question that best describes your current feelings about compassion.	ANSWER								Score	Weight	Total
1	Do you know what TJC integrity entails for self?	Y	S	N	NS						3	
2	How often do you make decisions with integrity for Self as a goal?**	D	W	M	Q	A	N	NS			3	
3	Are you aware of the times you elevate integrity for Self?	Y	S	N	NS						2	
4	Are you aware of the things you do that increase Integrity for Self?	Y	S	N	NS						2	
5	Do you feel accomplishment when you elevate integrity for Self?	Y	S	N	NS						3	
6	Do you create an environment of integrity for Self?	Y	S	N	NS						3	
7	Can you identify integrity in Others?	Y	S	N	NS						4	
8	Do you facilitate interactions with Others that model integrity?	Y	S	N	NS						4	
9	Do you start each day with the intention to increase integrity for Self and Others?	Y	S	N	NS						5	
10	Do you want more integrity in your life for Self and Others?	Y	S	N	NS						4	
11	Do you have the skill and tools required to elevate integrity in your life?	Y	S	N	NS						5	
12	Are you willing to dedicate your time and energy to elevate integrity?	Y	S	N	NS						5	

KEY Y=YES, S=SOMETIMES, N=NEVER, NS=NOT SURE
**DAILY/WEEKLY/MONTHLY/QUARTERLY/ANNUALLY/NEVER /NOT SURE (pick one)

Sum Total:
Sum Total /10:
New Total*2:
Round Totals Up or Down to Nearest Decimal

Key Score		Measurement Rules	Rankings
Y	6		49-52 Joyful +
N	1	In order to get the TJC Rank, multiply the Score column by the Weight column for each question.	44-48 Joyful
SOMETIMES	3	Enter that number in the Total column. Add the Total column and enter that number in to the Sum Total field.	39-43 Joyful -
NOT SURE	2	Divide the number in the Sum Total field by 10 and rounding up or down to the nearest decimal. Enter that	33-38 Neutral +
DAILY	6	number in the Sum Total / 10 field. Multiply the Sum Total / 10 field by 2, rounding up or down to nearest decimal.	27-32 Neutral
WEEKLY	5	Enter that number in the New Total*2 field. Compare that number to the Rankings and enter your ranking	16-26 Neutral -
MONTHLY	4	in the TJC Rank field at the top of the form. As an example, if I scored 39, I would write out Joyful-	≤ 15 Unhappy
QUARTERLY	3		
ANNUALLY	2		
NEVER	1		

BWWIY001.2   www.thejoycodex.com   Codex Capstone Media L.L.C.©

Take the Joy Codex Survey on days 1 and 7. You may take the survey all 7 days to get an extra little bit of boost as you start each day. The survey is a gage for you to understand your current feelings about integrity and will get you grounded in the new element you have just learned about. The measurement on the worksheet is a benchmark for you to increase your results based on your answers. You will know which areas to improve upon for the next day, you will be more focused.

The Joy Codex Elements In Action Integrity (Days 1-7) 1 copy used throughout the 7 days.

The Joy Codex Elements In Action		Integrity	
Elevate Integrity		**Little or No Integrity**	
1	Deep knowledge of personal values, ethics, morals, and spirituality.	1	Little knowledge of personal values, ethics, morals, and spirituality.
2	Doing the "right thing" all the time, even when no one is looking.	2	Doing the "incorrect thing" to benefit oneself.
3	Communicating with cognitive intention and integrity at all times.	3	Communicating with negative intent, causing pain, suffering, and resentment.
4	Cognitive Integrity, knowing thoughts influence emotions and behavior.	4	Not knowing or caring about how thoughts influence emotions and behavior.
5	Searching for solutions to improve the life of self and others.	5	No intention to improve the life of self and others.
6	Knowing that perfectionism is subjective and you do your best in all things.	6	Everyone must be perfect at all times.
7	Acting with the intention of integrity in all matters.	7	Acting without integrity.
8		8	
9		9	
10		10	
11		11	
12		12	
13		13	
14		14	
15		15	
16		16	

Use the spaces provided to add the items you have identified that elevate integrity and the items that don't. How do your thoughts influence your integrity with regard for self and others? How will you elevate integrity and what is the opposite of your action item, how will you know when it isn't demonstrated?

The Joy Codex Elements In Action worksheet challenges you to put your knowledge into action and to be cognitively aware when your actions are incongruent with The Joy Codex.

The Joy Codex Inventory Integrity (Days 1-7) 1 copy used throughout the 7 days.

The Joy Codex Inventory Integrity		
List the things you will do to elevate integrity for Self and Others.		
Self		Others

BWWIY0004.0   www.thejoycodex.com   Codex Capstone Media L.L.C.©

The Joy Codex Inventory is a list of the items/people/places/things that you do that demonstrate what you do for self and others within the given element.

The Joy Codex Quick Start Integrity (Days 1-7, at the start of your day) 7 copies.

THE JOY CODEX QUICK START   INTEGRITY

Name: Date: TJC Rank:

	Pick one answer per question that best describes your action plan for success today.	ANSWER				Score	Weight	Total
1	I know what TJC integrity entails for Self and Others today.	Y	S	N	NS		5	
2	I will elevate integrity for Self and Others today.	Y	S	N	NS		4	
3	I will act with integrity for Self and Others today.	Y	S	N	NS		3	
4	I will be aware of my ethics, morals, spirituality, and values in all actions with Self and Others today.	Y	S	N	NS		3	
5	I will knowingly make decisions that are in-line with my integrity today.	Y	S	N	NS		3	
6	I will place myself in situations with high levels of integrity today.	Y	S	N	NS		3	
7	I will respond to Others with integrity today.	Y	S	N	NS		4	
8	When I experience integrity for Self and Others today, I will be aware of that emotion.	Y	S	N	NS		4	
9	I will identify the interactions that elevate my integrity for Self and Others today.	Y	S	N	NS		5	
10	I will complete the Quick Wrap Integrity worksheet today.	Y	S	N	NS		4	
11	I will complete the SOaR worksheet today.	Y	S	N	NS		5	

Sum Total:
Sum Total /10:
New Total*2:

KEY Y=YES, S=SOMETIMES, N=NEVER, NS=NOT SURE

Round Totals Up or Down to Nearest Decimal

Key Score			Measurement Rules	Rankings
Y		6	In order to get the TJC Rank, multiply the Score column by the Weight column for each question.	49-52 Joyful +
N		1	Enter that number in the Total column. Add the Total column and enter that number in to the Sum Total field.	44-48 Joyful
SOMETIMES		3	Divide the number in the Sum Total field by 10 and rounding up or down to the nearest decimal. Enter that	39-43 Joyful -
NOT SURE		2	number in the Sum Total field. Multiply the Sum Total / 10 field by 2, rounding up or down to nearest decimal.	33-38 Neutral +
			Enter that number in the New Total*2 field. Compare that number to the Rankings and enter your ranking	27-32 Neutral
			in the TJC Rank field at the top of the form. As an example, if I scored 39, I would write out Joyful-	16-26 Neutral -
				≤ 15 Unhappy

BWWIY002.0   www.thejoycodex.com   Codex Capstone Media L.L.C.©

The Joy Codex Quick Start is an antecedent, the worksheet will prompt you at the start of your day to focus on specific points within the worksheet based on the unique element you are working on. This will be completed at the start of each day. The Quick Start worksheet has specific "I" statements to prepare your brain for success that day. The measurement on the form is a benchmark for you to increase your results based on your answers. You will know which areas to improve upon for the next day, you will be more focused.

The Joy Codex Quick Wrap Integrity (Days 1-7 at the end of your day) 7 copies.

THE JOY CODEX QUICK WRAP INTEGRITY

Name: _____ Date: _____ TJC Rank: _____

	Pick one answer per question that best describes your success for today.	ANSWER				Score	Weight	Total
1	Today I knew what TJC integrity meant for Self and Others.	Y	S	N	NS		5	
2	Today I elevated integrity for Self and Others.	Y	S	N	NS		4	
3	Today I acted with integrity for Self and Others.	Y	S	N	NS		3	
4	Today I will be aware of my ethics, morals, spirituality, and values in all actions with Self and Others.	Y	S	N	NS		3	
5	Today I knowingly make decisions that are in-line with my integrity.	Y	S	N	NS		3	
6	Today I placed myself in situations with high levels of integrity.	Y	S	N	NS		3	
7	Today I responded to Others with integrity.	Y	S	N	NS		4	
8	Today when I experienced integrity for Self and Others, I was aware of that emotion.	Y	S	N	NS		4	
9	Today I identified the interactions that elevated my integrity for Self and Others.	Y	S	N	NS		5	
10	Today I Completed the Quick Wrap Integrity worksheet.	Y	S	N	NS		4	
11	Today I completed the SOaR worksheet.	Y	S	N	NS		5	

KEY Y=YES, S=SOMETIMES, N=NEVER, NS=NOT SURE

Sum Total:
Sum Total /10:
New Total*2:

Round Totals Up or Down to Nearest Decimal

Key Score		Measurement Rules	Rankings
Y	6	In order to get the TJC Rank, multiply the Score column by the Weight column for each question.	49-52 Joyful +
N	1	Enter that number in the Total column. Add the Total column and enter that number in to the Sum Total field.	44-48 Joyful
SOMETIMES	3	Divide the Sum Total field by 10 and rounding up or down to the nearest decimal. Enter that	39-43 Joyful -
NOT SURE	2	number in the Sum Total / 10 field. Multiply the Sum Total / 10 field by 2, rounding up or down to nearest decimal	33-38 Neutral +
		Enter that number in the New Total*2 field. Compare that number to the Rankings and enter your ranking	27-32 Neutral
		in the TJC Rank field at the top of the form. As an example, if I scored 39, I would write out Joyful-	16-26 Neutral -
			≤ 15 Unhappy

BWW1Y003.1   www.thejoycodes.com   Codex Capstone Media L.L.C.©

The Joy Codex Quick Wrap worksheet is a review of your day specific to the element you are implementing. The questions are designed to stimulate your thought process about your day specific to each question and your application of the component. There is an expectation that you will review your day mentally and answer the questions thoughtfully. The measurement on the worksheet is a benchmark for you to know where you stand that day and to improve your results based on the questions to your answer and your rank. You will know which areas to improve upon for the next day, you will be more focused.

The Joy Codex SOaR Daily Log (Day 1-7 at the end of your day) 7 copies.

The Joy Codex SOaR Daily Log

Date	Rank (circle one icon that represents your day)	Score

Today I had a _____ day because _____
TJC RANK   the reasons you ranked Unhappy or Neutral or Joyful

Tomorrow I will _____
              detail the actions you will take to increase your success

TJC Rank
5 Unhappy   5   10   15   Name:
10 Neutral   Key Score   Rank:
15 Joyful

BWWBROOLO   www.thejoycodex.com   Codex Capstone Media L.L.C.

The Joy Codex SOaR Daily Log is a schedule of reinforcement. The form is very simple to use, there are three icons, ⊕ ⬜ ⬛ you will select the one that best represents how your day went in relation to applying the new skills and tools you are learning. From left to right the icons represent a day that required charging as you were unable to implement the element as desired. The middle icon represents a day that didn't go 100% as planned. You started your day with the Quick Start worksheet, you were cognizant of the specific items within each element, however, you found yourself slipping back into old behavior. The icon on the right is the full charge battery, this is a great day. You were completely aware of the Quick Start items that day and knew when you implemented them. The worksheet also has two statements from you; what the specific reasons were for your ranking that day, and a statement about what you will do specifically the next day to improve and succeed. The measurement on the worksheet is a benchmark for you to increase your results based on your answers. You will know which areas to improve upon for the next day, you will be more focused.

16 DEMONSTRATE RESPONSIBILITY

What is responsibility? Responsibility is a quality or state of being responsible (moral, legal, or mental accountability), reliable, trustworthy, something for which one is responsible

Demonstrate as an action word means to show clearly, to make clear by reasoning or evidence, and to show value. Demonstrating responsibility encompasses knowing that compassion and integrity are key drivers in achieving joy and self-actualization and being accountable to acting with purpose. When I demonstrate responsibility, I act.

Demonstrate	**Responsibility**

Demonstrate Responsibility is the third key and element to unlocking The Joy Codex and builds upon the elements of compassion and integrity.

There are two types of responsibility. Transactional responsibility, the rote actions that one does each day to physically survive and thrive. Cognitive responsibility is the more difficult one to achieve and the one that this element focuses on primarily.

Transactional responsibility is important, I clocked in on-time at work, I provided groceries for the family this week, I paid my bills on time, I worked out, I cleaned the house; or I put gas in the tank; these are all examples of transactional responsibility.

Within the context of The Joy Codex, demonstrating responsibility encompasses many additional mechanisms beyond transactional responsibility. Responsibility also includes acting (behavior) with compassion (feeling) and acting (behavior) with integrity(knowing). You have the knowledge and are responsible for acting (behavior) in a new way, The Joy Codex (TJC) way. You are now accountable to **act** on that **knowledge**.

Responsibility is not blaming others for your misery, suffering, or choices, and living with those choices **or making the necessary changes**. Responsibility for self, motivates me to engage in activities that increase my joy, confidence, and self-worth. When something in my life isn't going the way I want, I am responsible for the outcome and therefore I must act accordingly, making intelligent choices.

When I act, I'm cognizant of my compassion, integrity, and responsibility and I use the components of each element as instructed. In short, when I start to have negative thoughts about self and others, I know that I am off the mark and change my thoughts. I act in a way that will increase my joy.

Today when I hear people speaking poorly about themselves or another, I ask them how they are feeling about that situation, almost always the emotions are negative. If they are speaking negatively about self or others, their emotions will also be negative. I ask them how thinking negatively is working for them, are they happy and if the negative thoughts and behavior are getting them the results they want.

Demonstrating responsibility encompasses your actions, now that you "feel – compassion" and "know – integrity," you have a responsibility to self and others to "act – responsibly."

Responsibility entails listening to others, not thinking about what to say next and not interrupting. Listening with equal parts logic and emotion and responding intelligently. Minding the gap between a reaction and a response. Jumping to conclusions, guessing, inferring, or speculating about what a person thinks, feels, or intends without evidence or proof is a recipe for unhappiness and uncertainty.

I don't presume to know another's mind. I'm not a mind reader. I know I've made this statement a few times, however, it's an important lesson to learn. I'm not psychic, I can't tell the future, and I can't read minds. Knowing this, I have a responsibility to ask questions when I don't have all the answers and not fill in the blanks with assumptions.

Responsibility for self and others implies respect and strengthens interpersonal bonds and trust. To act responsibly within the context of TJC includes what we've learned, we understand and accept compassion, integrity, and responsibility for self and others.

Treating others with spite, resentment, anger, fear, and contempt doesn't serve me well, it doesn't feel good. In order to behave in this manner, I had to......I bet you know the answer! I had to think negative thoughts that increased negative emotions that amplified my negative behavior.

You now have a cognitive responsibility to interact positively, remember that bitching and complaining isn't conducive to increasing joy and is incongruent to joy.

I'm responsible for my thoughts about myself and others. I'm responsible for increasing my positive inner dialogue, this applies to self and others.

Responsibility to self and others doesn't mean taking inappropriate responsibility for other's actions. Responsibility isn't codependence, acting with responsibility entails compassion and integrity, codependence doesn't align with The Joy Codex methodology.

Being responsible for another's action is an act of irresponsibility toward oneself and decreases the likelihood others will assume responsibility. This is important for parents and managers of people; children and subordinates need responsibility demonstrated to them so that they may learn to develop self-confidence and healthy interpersonal relationships. Taking responsibility for others' issues, problems, and emotions may be a way to avoid our own issues and emotions.

We are not responsible for other's emotions and feelings; we are unable to interpret the world exactly as they do; through their filters. There isn't any way for us to know exactly how our words are interpreted and internalized by others. Communicating intentionally with compassion and integrity will mitigate some of the uncertainty.

Conversely others aren't responsible for our emotions and feelings. This might sound scary to some, however there should be a sense of relief that others aren't responsible for our emotions. We have complete responsibility for our emotions and feelings.

When I am commuting on the freeway and someone cuts me off, I initially have feelings of anger and irritation. I know that I am responsible for my feelings and rather than think negative horrible thoughts, increasing my frustration, I decide to change my negative thoughts and that changes my negative emotion.

The person that cut me off doesn't even know that I am angry or exist, they are long gone. They aren't thinking the negative thoughts or feeling the negative emotions that I am, so why do I want to feel them? Are those thoughts and emotions serving me well in my goal to increase joy?

They must've been in a hurry for a good reason, one that I don't know or understand. I don't want to give that person the power to dictate my emotions, they don't even know that they **had** that power. So, don't allow them any power or control over your emotions and joy.

Although I'm not responsible for other's emotions, I am responsible for my actions towards others. I don't expect everyone I meet to behave exactly as I do, I don't expect that they all have my integrity, compassion, or responsibility; I would like to prefer that.

Knowing that all people aren't self-actualized or have the same commitment to increasing joy, I have a responsibility to behave with the principals of The Joy Codex.

I've often heard the phrase **"energy flows where attention goes."** While in therapy that saying was altered slightly, **"where thoughts go, emotions flow."** Thoughts directly impact emotion. When I think negative thoughts about self, I quickly feel anxious, ashamed, frustrated, and depressed. When my thoughts about self are positive, I have feelings of self-worth and confidence. I am making a conscious decision to be responsible for my thoughts in order to increase my joy.

Demonstrating responsibility means that I'm an example to others by interacting free of manipulation, attention seeking, and resentment. When you interact with another, ask yourself, **"what do I want from this interaction and what is my intention with what I want."** It's easy to convince yourself that your intentions are good. In other words, it's easy to lie to yourself about your intentions.

Honesty with self becomes ever more important. If the emotion you are experiencing is negative and the verbiage you are employing is negative, resentful, hurtful, nasty, rude, unkind, uncompassionate or defensive, you aren't communicating responsibly. Go back and review what you want and what your intention is with that interaction. Act responsibly.

When I'm completely honest with myself about why I am interacting with an individual, and what my intention is, my behavior represents that; I'm behaving with responsibility.

Additionally, I'm not looking for others to validate my thoughts, emotions, and behavior, when I act with responsibility. I know that I'm acting with compassion, integrity, and responsibility. Quite frankly, I wouldn't want others to be responsible or validate my thoughts and emotions. I will be more aligned with my compassion, integrity, and responsibility for self. Demonstrating responsibility includes elevation of integrity and exemplification of compassion for self and others.

Boundary setting is important, I continue to write about boundaries as they have such an impact on **ensuring our needs are**

met and we don't become resentful. When we demonstrate responsibility we define, modify, implement, and remain firm with our boundaries; and those boundaries are implemented with the intent to improve relationships and increase joy.

When we set healthy boundaries that are implemented with compassion, integrity, and responsibility we are teaching others that there are limits to their behavior. I have a family member with a teenage daughter, there haven't been any boundaries between the parent and the child, there is a lack of respect for one another and they immediately speak to each other with contempt and resentment. The mother started implementing, communicating, and maintaining boundary lines, the child was not happy about the boundaries and for two weeks there was strife in the family. The child learned the new boundaries and the communication style has improved greatly. **Societally we interact with one another more clearly and effectively when we have clear communicated boundaries with one another**.

Here is another scenario, one of your family members or a roommate tells you that they don't want you to leave your dirty dishes in the sink and to place them in the dishwasher. They have set a boundary, most likely without knowing why or communicating the details. You start putting your dishes in the dishwasher after each use.

You notice that your family member or roommate keeps leaving their dirty dishes in the sink and you get irritated, they should **KNOW** better than to leave dirty dishes in the sink. They just asked you not to leave dirty dishes in the sink after all. Unless you specifically set that boundary and communicate that boundary with that family member or roommate, it doesn't exist. In your mind it might exist, and it seems like common decency, if they asked you to place the dirty dishes in the dishwasher, they should do the same. Unfortunately, when others are setting boundaries intentionally or not, they are getting their needs met, when you don't set boundaries your needs aren't being met.

Barriers to Success

This element has the biggest barrier to success. This is where apathy really comes into play, especially for neutral people. The demonstrate responsibility element is where the rubber hits the road, this is where you are required to act on what you know.

This is often where the excuses start. Beware, if you are **making excuses** to yourself about why you aren't acting responsibly, with the elements of compassion and integrity included. You will need to do some soul searching and determine if you are ready to make the changes required to live a life of joy. Blaming others is also a major barrier to success. The bottom line is that you want to increase joy consistently, excuses and blame won't get you closer to the goal.

Final Thoughts

When I demonstrate responsibility, I act. Demonstrating responsibility encompasses knowing that compassion and integrity are key drivers in achieving joy, self-actualization, and being accountable to acting with purpose. Transactional responsibility is important, cognitive responsibility is even more important. When you act with cognitive responsibility you are planning your actions with compassion and integrity.

Ownership of your actions and not blaming others for your pain and suffering is critical to your success. No victims here! Responsibility for your behavior means that you are responsible for your thoughts and emotions; and you act accordingly.

Complete honesty when answering the worksheets demonstrates responsibility. A score achieved through dishonesty only serves to reduce joy, the score isn't a competition. When you know what your score is from day to day, you have the ability to make changes that will increase your score the following day.

Now that you've completed the chapter on responsibility, it's time to put what you've learned into action! Again, this is the fun part! Know that you are making intelligent choices combined with intention and action to achieve a goal.

Worksheets

Applying responsibility to self and others is a learned behavior and available to everyone. Let's get started, all forms are online at www.thejoycodex.com/forms

The worksheets are for you, this is your information, how you feel and what you think. There aren't any right or wrong answers, the rank is there to give you a consistent measurement of where you are for that category at that moment allowing you to improve.

Print enough copies of each worksheet based on the instructions below. For best results follow the directions exactly.

At the end of the book, there are additional worksheets that may be of value to you today. Please review these worksheets and determine if they are applicable for that moment. The worksheets are the "SOaR Monthly," "What Element Could I Have Applied," "Change My Thoughts, Emotions, Behaviors" "Thoughts, Emotions, Behaviors," and "The Behavior I want, via, Thought and Emotion."

The Joy Codex Survey Responsibility (Days 1 and 7) 2 copies.

THE JOY CODEX SURVEY — RESPONSIBILITY

Name: _____ Date: _____ TJC Rank: _____

	Pick one answer per question that best describes your current feelings about responsibility.	ANSWER								Score	Weight	Total
1	Do you know what cognitive responsibility for Self entails?	Y	S	N	NS						3	
2	How often do you act with cognitively responsibly for Self?**	D	W	M	Q	A	N	NS			3	
3	Are you aware of those moments that you act responsibly for Self, both transactionally and cognitively?	Y	S	N	NS						2	
4	Does your behavior increase cognitive responsibility for Self?	Y	S	N	NS						2	
5	Do you demonstrate cognitive responsibility for Self?	Y	S	N	NS						3	
6	Do you set healthy boundaries with responsibility for Self?	Y	S	N	NS						3	
7	Do you act with cognitive responsibility when interacting with Others?	Y	S	N	NS						4	
8	Do you communicate with positive intention for Others?	Y	S	N	NS						4	
9	Do you start each day with the intention to demonstrate responsibility for Self and Others?	Y	S	N	NS						5	
10	Do you want to act with cognitive responsibility for Self and Others?	Y	S	N	NS						4	
11	Do you have the skill and tools to increase cognitive responsibility in your life?	Y	S	N	NS						5	
12	Are you willing to dedicate your time and energy to increasing your responsibility?	Y	S	N	NS						5	

KEY Y=YES, S=SOMETIMES, N=NEVER, NS=NOT SURE

**DAILY/WEEKLY/MONTHLY/QUARTERLY/ANNUALLY/NEVER /NOT SURE (pick one)

Sum Total: _____
Sum Total /10: _____
New Total*2: _____

Round Totals Up or Down to Nearest Decimal

Key Score		Measurement Rules	Rankings
Y	6	In order to get the TJC Rank, multiply the Score column by the Weight column for each question.	49-52 Joyful +
N	1	Enter that number in the Total column. Add the Total column and enter that number in to the Sum Total field.	44-48 Joyful
SOMETIMES	3	Divide the number in the Sum Total field by 10 and rounding up or down to the nearest decimal. Enter that	39-43 Joyful -
NOT SURE	2	number in the Sum Total / 10 field. Multiply the Sum Total / 10 field by 2, rounding up or down to nearest decimal.	33-38 Neutral +
DAILY	6	Enter that number in the New Total*2 field. Compare that number to the Rankings and enter your ranking	26-32 Neutral
WEEKLY	5	in the TJC Rank field at the top of the form. As an example, if I scored 39, I would write out Joyful-	16-26 Neutral -
MONTHLY	4		≤ 15 Unhappy
QUARTERLY	3		
ANNUALLY	2		
NEVER	1		

BWWRY001.0 — www.thejoycodex.com — Codex Capstone Media L.L.C.©

Take the Joy Codex Survey on days 1 and 7. You may take the survey all 7 days to get an extra little bit of boost as you start each day. The survey is a gage for you to understand your current feelings about responsibility and will get you grounded in the new element you have just learned about. The measurement on the worksheet is a benchmark for you to increase your results based on your answers. You will know which areas to improve upon for the next day, you will be more focused.

The Joy Codex Elements In Action Responsibility (Days 1-7) 1 copy used throughout the 7 days.

The Joy Codex Elements In Action — Responsibility	
Demonstrate Responsibility	**Acting with Irresponsibility**
1 Acting with your knowledge of compassion and integrity for Self and Others.	1 Acting with cognitive irresponsibility, knowingly for Self and Others.
2 Engage in activities that increase joy, confidence, and self-worth.	2 Engage in activities that decrease joy, confidence, and self-worth.
3 Think with cognitive responsibility in order to influence emotion and behavior.	3 No concern for how thinking influences emotion and behavior.
4 Acting with transactional responsibility.	4 Acting with transactional irresponsibility.
5 Minding the gap in order to RESPOND rather than react.	5 Immediately REACTING without cognitive responsibility.
6 Treating Self and Others with kindness, patience, compassion, and integrity.	6 Treating Self and Others with spite, resentment, anger, fear, and contempt
7 Acting with cognitive responsibility in all matters.	7 Acting without cognitive responsibility.
8	8
9	9
10	10
11	11
12	12
13	13
14	14
15	15
16	16

Use the spaces provided to add the items you have identified that demonstrate responsibility and the items that don't. How do your thoughts influence your cognitive responsibility with regard to self and others? How will you demonstrate responsibility and what is the opposite of your action item, how will you know when it isn't demonstrated?

BWWRY005.2   www.thejoycodex.com   Codex Capstone Media L.L.C.©

The Joy Codex Elements In Action worksheet challenges you to put your knowledge into action and to be cognitively aware when your actions are incongruent with The Joy Codex.

The Joy Codex Inventory Responsibility (Days 1-7) 1 copy used throughout the 7 days.

The Joy Codex Inventory Repsonsibility

List the things that demonstrate responsibility for Self and Others.

Self	Others
1	1
2	2
3	3
4	4
5	5
6	6
7	7
8	8
9	9
10	10
11	11
12	12
13	13
14	14
15	15
16	16
17	17
18	18
19	19
20	20

BWWRY0004.0   www.thejoycodex.com   Codex Capstone Media L.L.C.

The Joy Codex Inventory is a list of the items/people/places/things that you do that demonstrate what you do for self and others within the given element.

The Joy Codex Quick Start Responsibility (Days 1-7, at the start of your day) 7 copies.

THE JOY CODEX QUICK START — RESPONSIBILITY

Name: _____ Date: _____ TJC Rank: _____

	Pick one answer per question that best describes your action plan for success today.	ANSWER				Score	Weight	Total
1	I know what TJC responsibility entails for Self and Others today.	Y	S	N	NS		5	
2	I will act with cognitive responsibility for Self today.**	Y	S	N	NS		4	
3	I will demonstrate responsibility for Self and Others today.	Y	S	N	NS		3	
4	I will act with responsibility, both transactionally and cognitively for Self and Others today.	Y	S	N	NS		3	
5	I will incorporate the elements of compassion and integrity for Self and Others today.	Y	S	N	NS		3	
6	I will be aware of those moments that I act responsibly for Self and Others, both transactionally and cognitively.	Y	S	N	NS		3	
7	I will set healthy boundaries with positive intent and responsibility for Self and Others today.	Y	S	N	NS		4	
8	I will communicate with positive intention for Self and Others today.	Y	S	N	NS		4	
9	I will identify the interactions that demonstrate cognitive responsibility for Self and Others today.	Y	S	N	NS		5	
10	I will complete the Quick Wrap Responsibility worksheet today.	Y	S	N	NS		4	
11	I will complete the SOaR worksheet today.	Y	S	N	NS		5	

Sum Total:

Sum Total /10:

New Total*2:

Round Totals Up or Down to Nearest Decimal

KEY Y=YES, S=SOMETIMES, N=NEVER, NS=NOT SURE

Key Score		Measurement Rules	Rankings
Y	6	In order to get the TJC Rank, multiply the Score column by the Weight column for each question.	49-52 Joyful +
N	1	Enter that number in the Total column. Add the Total column and enter that number in to the Sum Total field.	44-48 Joyful
SOMETIMES	3	Divide the number in the Sum Total field by 10 and rounding up or down to the nearest decimal. Enter that	39-43 Joyful -
NOT SURE	2	number in the Sum Total / 10 field. Multiply the Sum Total / 10 field by 2, rounding up or down to nearest decimal.	33-38 Neutral +
		Enter that number in the New Total*2 field. Compare that number to the Rankings and enter your ranking	27-32 Neutral
		in the TJC Rank field at the top of the form. As an example, if I scored 39, I would write out Joyful-	16-26 Neutral -
			≤ 15 Unhappy

BWWRY002.0 — www.thejoycodex.com — Codex Capstone Media L.L.C.©

The Joy Codex Quick Start is an antecedent, the worksheet will prompt you at the start of your day to focus on specific points within the worksheet based on the unique element you are working on. This will be completed at the start of each day. The Quick Start worksheet has specific "I" statements to prepare your brain for success that day. The measurement on the form is a benchmark for you to increase your results based on your answers. You will know which areas to improve upon for the next day, you will be more focused.

The Joy Codex Quick Wrap Responsibility (Days 1-7 at the end of your day) 7 copies.

THE JOY CODEX QUICK WRAP — RESPONSIBILITY

Name: _____ Date: _____ TJC Rank: _____

	Pick one answer per question that best describes your success for today.	ANSWER				Score	Weight	Total
1	Today I knew what TJC responsibility entailed for Self and Others.	Y	S	N	NS		5	
2	Today I acted with cognitively responsibly for Self.	Y	S	N	NS		4	
3	Today I demonstrated responsibility for Self and Others.	Y	S	N	NS		3	
4	Today I acted with responsibility, both transactionally and cognitively for Self and Others.	Y	S	N	NS		3	
5	Today I incorporated the elements of compassion and integrity for Self and Others today.	Y	S	N	NS		3	
6	Today I was aware of the moments that I acted responsibly for Self and Others, both transactionally and cognitively.	Y	S	N	NS		3	
7	Today I set healthy boundaries with positive intent and responsibility for Self and Others, when applicable..	Y	S	N	NS		4	
8	Today I communicated with positive intention for Self and Others.	Y	S	N	NS		4	
9	Today I identified the interactions that demonstrated cognitive responsibility for Self and Others.	Y	S	N	NS		5	
10	Today I Completed the Quick Wrap Integrity worksheet.	Y	S	N	NS		4	
11	Today I completed the SOaR worksheet.	Y	S	N	NS		5	

KEY Y=YES, S=SOMETIMES, N=NEVER, NS=NOT SURE

Sum Total:
Sum Total /10:
New Total*2:
Round Totals Up or Down to Nearest Decimal

Key Score		Measurement Rules	Rankings
Y	6	In order to get the TJC Rank, multiply the Score column by the Weight column for each question.	49-52 Joyful +
N	1	Enter that number in the Total column. Add the Total column and enter that number in to the Sum Total field.	44-48 Joyful
SOMETIMES	3	Divide the number in the Sum Total field by 10 and rounding up or down to the nearest decimal. Enter that	39-43 Joyful -
NOT SURE	2	number in the Sum Total / 10 field. Multiply the Sum Total / 10 field by 2, rounding up or down to nearest decimal	33-38 Neutral +
		Enter that number in the New Total*2 field. Compare that number to the Rankings and enter your ranking	27-32 Neutral
		in the TJC Rank field at the top of the form. As an example, if I scored 39, I would write out Joyful-	16-26 Neutral -
			≤ 15 Unhappy

BWWRY003.0   www.thejoycodex.com   Codex Capstone Media L.L.C.©

The Joy Codex Quick Wrap worksheet is a review of your day specific to the element you are implementing. The questions are designed to stimulate your thought process about your day specific to each question and your application of the component. There is an expectation that you will review your day mentally and answer the questions thoughtfully. The measurement on the worksheet is a benchmark for you to increase your results based on your answers. You will know which areas to improve upon for the next day, you will be more focused.

The Joy Codex SOaR Daily Log (Day 1-7 at the end of your day) 7 copies.

The Joy Codex SOaR Daily Log

Date — Rank (circle one icon that represents your day) — Score

Today I had a _____ day because _____
TJC RANK — the reasons you ranked Unhappy or Neutral or Joyful

Tomorrow I will _____
detail the actions you will take to increase your success

TJC Rank
5 Unhappy
10 Neutral
15 Joyful

5 — 10 — 15
Key Score

Name:
Rank:

©WWBRD010 — www.thejoycodex.com — Codex Capstone Media L.L.C.

The Joy Codex SOaR Daily Log is a schedule of reinforcement. The form is very simple to use, there are three icons, ⚡ ▢ ▮ you will select the one that best represents how your day went in relation to applying the new skills and tools you are learning. From left to right the icons represent a day that required charging as you were unable to implement the element as desired. The middle icon represents a day that didn't go 100% as planned. You started your day with the Quick Start worksheet, you were cognizant of the specific items within each element, however, you found yourself slipping back into old behavior. The icon on the right is the full charge battery, this is a great day. You were completely aware of the Quick Start items that day and knew when you implemented them. The worksheet also has two statements from you; what the specific reasons were for your ranking that day, and a statement about what you will do specifically the next day to improve and succeed. The measurement on the worksheet is a benchmark for you to increase your results based on your answers. You will know which areas to improve upon for the next day, you will be more focused.

17 OPERATE WITH CLARITY

What is clarity? Clarity is the quality or state of being clear, coherent, intelligible and transparent.

Operate as an action word means to perform a function, to produce an appropriate effect, and to perform a series of functions. When operating with clarity you are acting intelligently, behaving with the intention to achieve a purpose, you measure your results to determine effectiveness and make changes. When I operate with clarity, I measure.

Operate w/ **CLARITY**

Operate with Clarity is the fourth element and key to unlocking The Joy Codex. Clarity builds on the elements of responsibility, integrity, and compassion. **Having clarity for self and others means being cognitively and emotionally sound in your decisions and the actions you take to improve your life and those around you.**

Clarity for self and others is also fundamental to succeeding in your desire to increase joy.

Again, operating with clarity encompasses instituting and implementing clear, coherent, and intelligible thoughts, emotions and behaviors, in order to achieve an outcome that increases joy for self and others. Operating with clarity also encompasses awareness, knowing if your actions are making the improvements you are implementing, a measurement.

What do you want? Why are you reading this book? Are you clear, coherent, and intelligible about what you want? Do you know what steps to take in order to reach your goal? How will you know when you reach your goal?

I don't often encounter individuals that can clearly elucidate what they want, the steps required to achieve their goal, if they were successful, or how they will sustain change.

For arguments sake, let's say that you want to increase your joy, that is why you are reading this book. The Joy Codex methodology is about increasing joy via a defined set of steps with the measurement and reinforcement built in. You have made a clear and intelligible decision to take the action required to improve, and you are operating with clarity. You know what you want; you know how to achieve that goal; you will know when you are successful, and you will sustain.

Operating with clarity is a conscious decision to speak and act in a manner that is conducive to increasing joy. **Clarity of thought for self and others, includes thinking positively about self and others as this increases positive emotions and behavior.**

Clarity in my communications, knowing that my words to self and others will have an impact means that I have a responsibility to act in such a way as to increase the positive result.

When you communicate with clarity, you know what you want to say, you know what your intention is, you choose verbiage that conveys your message clearly and with positive intent.

Communicating with cognitive clarity also entails speaking with an even balance of logic and emotion.

Being clear, concise, and acting with intelligence to achieve a purpose isn't as easy as it sounds. Now that you have compassion, integrity, and responsibility for self and others; you also need clarity and consistency. Waking up each day with the clarity to intentionally increase joy.

Clarity for others means that I communicate clearly with intent to convey compassion and integrity; I have a responsibility. My behavior, and the decisions I make regarding others, includes knowing my actions impact others. Say what you mean and mean what you say.

Minding the gap is important for clarity of thought. **Clarity of thought leads to clarity in emotion and behavior.** Remember, minding the gap is the difference between reacting to a situation versus responding to a situation. When I'm in a heated conversation, I'm taking that extra millisecond before I respond, to have clarity of intention in the words I convey knowing they will be conveyed with compassion, integrity, and responsibility.

When interacting with a person that is goading you, remember your compassion, integrity, responsibility, and clarity. If you get heated, <u>you choose to accept</u> the gift they are giving you, emotional chaos. Reject the gift and extend the gap and **respond in a way that increases your joy**.

Hint, when communicating with others that aren't clear and are over-emotional, slow the conversation (extend the gap between a reaction and a response), take emotion off the table for a moment, and define the issue clearly. Don't mix the issues, handle multiple issues one at a time, and separately. What is the other person attempting to accomplish, what is their need at that moment, what is their intent?

When I'm communicating with another that lacks clarity, I **ask leading questions to gain a better understanding** of what they think I said or what they think I intended to communicate. This gives me an opportunity to present my statements in the way that I intended, and this allows me to select verbiage to be more direct and clearer with another.

How do you know if the things you are doing are getting you the results you want? Do you implement a new skill and test each component to determine the results? Is it important for you to know if you are succeeding? Do you measure your results and apply intelligent action to improve your results? The answer for today, is yes, because you have been implementing The Joy Codex. You are aware of how your actions directly impact your results. You've measured your results and initiated specific actions to improve; and continue to measure and improve.

I specifically added measurement and reinforcement to The Joy Codex to increase the desired behavior. The reinforcement causes an increase in behavior and the measurement scores the current state. There is still a need for you to be steadfast and invested in the process and have a deep commitment to a more joyful and complete life.

Clarity and boundaries go hand in hand. If you aren't clear on the things that bother you or what your limits are, how will you share those requirements and needs with others? Others aren't mind readers, they may claim to be, however, they didn't live the exact same life as you and have different filters to view and interpret the world.

Remember when you are feeling anxious and uncomfortable or resentful seeing or hearing another's behavior, a boundary needs to be set. Be clear cognitively and emotionally about the boundaries you implement, know the specifics so that you know when a boundary is being crossed. Be clear about how you will communicate the boundary when set and when crossed.

Barriers to Success

Laziness may be an issue for those that have a desire to improve their clarity. **Operating with clarity involves dedication, commitment, and action; an apathetic attitude is a hinderance.**

People that lack clarity for self or others can be disorganized or appear to go with the flow, not really having an opinion. **Knowing what you want, how to get what you want, and acting appropriately on those wants are indicators that a person is operating with clarity.**

I'm sure it comes as no surprise to you that alcohol and mind-altering substance use are barriers to cognitive clarity. If you are unable to regulate your thoughts and emotions due to consumption, you are unable to increase cognitive clarity. This is a choice.

Cognitive clarity requires a responsibility to act in ways that increase your joy. Most importantly, clarity is knowing what you want, having a plan, and measuring that success. How do you know if you are succeeding unless you are clear?

Final Thoughts

When I operate with clarity, I measure. Measurement is an important component of The Joy Codex. How do you know if you are achieving your goal if you don't know the score? Awareness of where you stand on compassion, integrity, and responsibility will help you operate with clarity.

As you've utilized the worksheets you've been measuring your success. You have cognitive clarity about the areas you want to improve, and you've initiated an action plan via The Joy Codex. You know where you stand by consistent measurement, and you are clear on your next steps to achieve your goal of increased joy.

Complete honesty when answering the worksheets demonstrates that you are operating with clarity. A score achieved through dishonesty only serves to exacerbate your unhappiness, the score isn't a competition. When you know what your score is from day to day, you have the ability to make specific changes that will increase your score the following day.

Now that you've completed the chapter on clarity, it's time to put what learned into action! Again, this is the fun part! Know that you are making intelligent choices combined with intention and action to achieve a goal.

Worksheets

Fortunately, operating with clarity for self and others is a learned behavior and available to everyone. Let's get started, all forms are online at www.thejoycodex.com/forms

The worksheets are for you, this is your information, how you feel and what you think. There aren't any right or wrong answers, the rank is there to give you a consistent measurement of where you are for that category at that moment, allowing you to improve.

Print enough copies of each worksheet based on the instructions below. For best results follow the directions exactly.

At the end of the book, there are additional worksheets that may be of value to you today. Please review these worksheets and determine if they are applicable for that moment. The worksheets are the "SOaR Monthly," "What Element Could I Have Applied," "Change My Thoughts, Emotions, Behaviors" "Thoughts, Emotions, Behaviors," and "The Behavior I want, via, Thought and Emotion."

The Joy Codex Survey Clarity (Days 1 and 7) 2 copies.

THE JOY CODEX SURVEY CLARITY

Name: _____ Date: _____ TJC Rank: _____

	Pick one answer per question that best describes your current feelings about clarity.	ANSWER								Score	Weight	Total
1	Do you know what cognitive clarity for Self entails?	Y	S	N	NS						3	
2	How often do you act with cognitively clarity for Self?**	D	W	M	Q	A	N	NS			3	
3	Are you aware of those moments that you act with clarity for Self?	Y	S	N	NS						2	
4	Does your behavior increase cognitive clarity for Self?	Y	S	N	NS						2	
5	Do you know if your actions are achieving the results you want?	Y	S	N	NS						3	
6	Do you measure your success?	Y	S	N	NS						3	
7	Do you act with cognitive clarity when interacting with Others?	Y	S	N	NS						4	
8	Do you communicate with clarity and intention for Others?	Y	S	N	NS						4	
9	Do you start each day with the intention to operate with integrity for Self and Others?	Y	S	N	NS						5	
10	Do you want to act with cognitive clarity for Self and Others?	Y	S	N	NS						4	
11	Do you have the skill and tools to increase cognitive clarity in your life?	Y	S	N	NS						5	
12	Are you willing to dedicate your time and energy to increasing your responsibility?	Y	S	N	NS						5	

Sum Total: _____

KEY Y=YES, S=SOMETIMES, N=NEVER, NS=NOT SURE

**DAILY/WEEKLY/MONTHLY/QUARTERLY/ANNUALLY/NEVER /NOT SURE (pick one)

Sum Total /10: _____

New Total*2: _____

Round Totals Up or Down to Nearest Decimal

Key Score		Measurement Rules	Rankings
Y	6	In order to get the TJC Rank, multiply the Score column by the Weight column for each question.	49-52 Joyful +
N	1	Enter that number in the Total column. Add the Total column and enter that number in to the Sum Total field.	44-48 Joyful
SOMETIMES	3	Divide the number in the Sum Total field by 10 and rounding up or down to the nearest decimal. Enter that	39-43 Joyful -
NOT SURE	2	number in the Sum Total / 10 field. Multiply the Sum Total / 10 field by 2, rounding up or down to nearest decimal.	33-38 Neutral +
DAILY	6	Enter that number in the New Total*2 field. Compare that number to the Rankings and enter your ranking	26-32 Neutral
WEEKLY	5	in the TJC Rank field at the top of the form. As an example, if I scored 39, I would write out Joyful-	16-26 Neutral -
MONTHLY	4		≤ 15 Unhappy
QUARTERLY	3		
ANNUALLY	2		
NEVER	1		

BWWCY001.0   www.thejoycodex.com   Codex Capstone Media L.L.C.©

Take the Joy Codex Survey on days 1 and 7. You may take the survey all 7 days to get an extra little bit of boost as you start each day. The survey is a gage for you to understand your current feelings about clarity and will get you grounded in the new element you have just learned about. The measurement on the worksheet is a benchmark for you to increase your results based on your answers. You will know which areas to improve upon for the next day, you will be more focused.

The Joy Codex Elements In Action Clarity (Days 1-7) 1 copy used throughout the 7 days.

The Joy Codex Elements In Action Clarity		
Operate w/ Clarity		**Lack of Clarity**
1	Knowing where you stand in your journey for well-being.	1	Not being sure that there is or was a journey.
2	Measuring your success in order to determine next steps.	2	Not clear cognitively, no plan in place to measure success.
3	Communicating with cognitive clarity, an even balance of logic and emotion.	3	Communicating with an over-abundance or logic and emotion.
4	Cognitive clarity of thought, leads to clarity in emotion and behavior.	4	Disregard for cognitive clarity leading to negative thought, emotion, and behavior.
5	Actions that are aligned with cognitive clarity.	5	Actions without clear intention.
6	Knowing what you want, the steps required, and acting with cognitive intention.	6	Not being clear with your wants, the steps required and lack of action.
7	Setting healthy clear boundaries and communicating those boundaries clearly.	7	Unaware of boundaries, lack of boundaries, lack of communicating boundaries.
8		8	
9		9	
10		10	
11		11	
12		12	
13		13	
14		14	
15		15	
16		16	

Use the spaces provided to add the items you have identified showing you operate w/ clarity and the items that don't. How do your thoughts influence your clarity with regard to self and others? How will you operate w/ clarity and what is the opposite of your action item, how will you know when it isn't demonstrated?

BWWCY005.0   www.thejoycodex.com   Codex Capstone Media L.L.C.©

The Joy Codex Elements In Action worksheet challenges you to put your knowledge into action and to be cognitively aware when your actions are incongruent with The Joy Codex.

The Joy Codex Inventory Responsibility (Days 1-7) 1 copy used throughout the 7 days.

The Joy Codex Inventory Clarity

List the things you will do to operate with clarity for Self and Others.

Self	Others
1	1
2	2
3	3
4	4
5	5
6	6
7	7
8	8
9	9
10	10
11	11
12	12
13	13
14	14
15	15
16	16
17	17
18	18
19	19
20	20

BWWCY0004.0   www.thejoycodex.com   Codex Capstone Media L.L.C.©

The Joy Codex Inventory is a list of the items/people/places/things that you do that demonstrate what you do for self and others within the given element.

The Joy Codex Quick Start Clarity (Days 1-7, at the start of your day) 7 copies.

THE JOY CODEX QUICK START				CLARITY				
Name:	Date:	TJC Rank:						
Pick one answer per question that best describes your action plan for success today.				ANSWER		Score	Weight	Total
1	I know what TJC clarity entails for Self and Others today.			Y S N NS			5	
2	I will operate with clarity for Self and Others today.**			Y S N NS			4	
3	I will measure my performance as it relates to TJC today.			Y S N NS			3	
4	I will mind the gap with intelligence and clarity today.			Y S N NS			3	
5	I will incorporate the elements of compassion, integrity, responsibility, and clarity for Self and Others today.			Y S N NS			3	
6	I will be aware of those moments that I operate with clarity for Self and Others today.			Y S N NS			3	
7	I will set healthy boundaries with positive intent and clarity today, when applicable.			Y S N NS			4	
8	I will communicate with positive intention and clarity for Self and Others today.			Y S N NS			4	
9	I will identify the interactions that exhibit cognitive clarity for Self and Others today.			Y S N NS			5	
10	I will complete the Quick Wrap Clarity worksheet today.			Y S N NS			4	
11	I will complete the SOaR worksheet today.			Y S N NS			5	
						Sum Total:		
	KEY Y=YES, S=SOMETIMES, N=NEVER, NS=NOT SURE					Sum Total /10:		
						New Total*2:		
						Round Totals Up or Down to Nearest Decimal		

Key Score			Measurement Rules	Rankings
Y		6	In order to get the TJC Rank, multiply the Score column by the Weight column for each question.	49-52 Joyful +
N		1	Enter that number in the Total column. Add the Total column and enter that number in to the Sum Total field.	44-48 Joyful
SOMETIMES		3	Divide the number in the Sum Total field by 10 and rounding up or down to the nearest decimal. Enter that	39-43 Joyful -
NOT SURE		2	number in the Sum Total / 10 field. Multiply the Sum Total / 10 field by 2, rounding up or down to nearest decimal.	33-38 Neutral +
			Enter that number in the New Total*2 field. Compare that number to the Rankings and enter your ranking	27-32 Neutral
			in the TJC Rank field at the top of the form. As an example, if I scored 39, I would write out Joyful-	16-26 Neutral -
				≤ 15 Unhappy
BWWCY002.0			www.thejoycodex.com	Codex Capstone Media L.L.C.©

The Joy Codex Quick Start is an antecedent, the worksheet will prompt you at the start of your day to focus on specific points within the worksheet based on the unique element you are working on. This will be completed at the start of each day. The Quick Start worksheet has specific "I" statements to prepare your brain for success that day. The measurement on the form is a benchmark for you to increase your results based on your answers. You will know which areas to improve upon for the next day, you will be more focused.

The Joy Codex Quick Wrap Clarity (Days 1-7 at the end of your day) 7 copies.

THE JOY CODEX QUICK WRAP   CLARITY

Name: _____ Date: _____ TJC Rank: _____

	Pick one answer per question that best describes your success for today.	ANSWER				Score	Weight	Total
1	Today I knew what TJC clarity was for Self and Others.	Y	S	N	NS		5	
2	Today I acted with cognitive clarity for Self and Others.	Y	S	N	NS		4	
3	Today I measured my performance as it relates to TJC.	Y	S	N	NS		3	
4	Today I was able to mind the gap with intelligence and clarity.	Y	S	N	NS		3	
5	Today I incorporated the elements of compassion, integrity, responsibility, and clarity for Self and Others.	Y	S	N	NS		3	
6	Today I was aware of those moments that I operated with clarity for Self and Others.	Y	S	N	NS		3	
7	Today I set healthy boundaries with positive intent and clarity when applicable.	Y	S	N	NS		4	
8	Today I communicated with positive intent and clarity for Self and Others.	Y	S	N	NS		4	
9	Today I identified the interactions that exhibited cognitive clarity for Self and Others.	Y	S	N	NS		5	
10	Today I Completed the Quick Wrap Clarity worksheet.	Y	S	N	NS		4	
11	Today I completed the SOaR worksheet.	Y	S	N	NS		5	

Sum Total:
KEY Y=YES, S=SOMETIMES, N=NEVER, NS=NOT SURE   Sum Total /10:
New Total*2:
Round Totals Up or Down to Nearest Decimal

Key Score		Measurement Rules	Rankings
Y	6	In order to get the TJC Rank, multiply the Score column by the Weight column for each question.	49-52 Joyful +
N	1	Enter that number in the Total column. Add the Total column and enter that number in to the Sum Total field.	44-48 Joyful
SOMETIMES	3	Divide the number in the Sum Total field by 10 and rounding up or down to the nearest decimal. Enter that	39-43 Joyful -
NOT SURE	2	number in the Sum Total / 10 field. Multiply the Sum Total / 10 field by 2, rounding up or down to nearest decimal.	33-38 Neutral +
		Enter that number in the New Total*2 field. Compare that number to the Rankings and enter your ranking	26-32 Neutral
		in the TJC Rank field at the top of the form. As an example, if I scored 39, I would write out Joyful-	16-26 Neutral -
			≤ 15 Unhappy

BWWCY003.0   www.thejoycodex.com   Codex Capstone Media L.L.C ©

The Joy Codex Quick Wrap worksheet is a review of your day specific to the element you are implementing. The questions are designed to stimulate your thought process about your day specific to each question and your application of the component. There is an expectation that you will review your day mentally and answer the questions thoughtfully. The measurement on the worksheet is a benchmark for you to increase your results based on your answers. You will know which areas to improve upon for the next day, you will be more focused.

The Joy Codex SOaR Daily Log (Day 1-7 at the end of your day) 7 copies.

The Joy Codex SOaR Daily Log is a schedule of reinforcement. The form is very simple to use, there are three icons, [battery icons] you will select the one that best represents how your day went in relation to applying the new skills and tools you are learning. From left to right the icons represent a day that required charging as you were unable to implement the element as desired. The middle icon represents a day that didn't go 100% as planned. You started your day with the Quick Start worksheet, you were cognizant of the specific items within each element, however, you found yourself slipping back into old behavior. The icon on the right is the full charge battery, this is a great day. You were completely aware of the Quick Start items that day and knew when you implemented them. The worksheet also has two statements from you; what the specific reasons were for your ranking that day, and a statement about what you will do specifically the next day to improve and succeed. The measurement on the worksheet is a benchmark for you to increase your results based on your answers. You will know which areas to improve upon for the next day, you will be more focused.

18 CHOOSE JOY

What is joy? Joy is an emotional state that is characterized by feelings of elation, euphoria, ecstasy, delight, happiness, jubilation, gratification, pleasure, satisfaction, and well-being.

Choose as an action word means to select after consideration, to decide, to plan and to have a preference. Choose joy encompasses a decision, a plan, and after careful consideration, implementation with the intention to improve and increase feelings of joy. When I choose joy for self and others; I improve.

Choose

JOY

Choose Joy is the fifth element and final key to unlocking and solving The Joy Codex. Joy is also the capstone for The Joy Codex Method.

Before we jump into the chapter let's try a quick breathing exercise, **if you are operating heavy machinery or if you are otherwise incapacitated, please refrain from this exercise until convenient.** Directions: You will breathe in through your nose for five seconds and hold it, and then you will breathe out through your mouth for seven seconds. While you are breathing air in through your nose, imagine that the air is filled with a sense of joy, allow that joy to spread over your chest, through your heart and flow throughout your body. When you breathe out through your mouth, imagine that you are releasing that joy out into the world.

You will do this a total of three times, the second and third time, as you breathe in say to yourself, "I breathe in joy" and as you exhale, say "I breathe out joy." Feel that joy, a sense of peace and well-being.

When ready, close your eyes, breathe in through your nose for five seconds and hold it, breathe out through your mouth for seven seconds following the directions above. I Always feel better after that exercise.

Did you feel joy? What did that joy feel like? Did you like that feeling? Let's explore joy.

Joyful is a state of being, and not a moment. Moments are joyous, you are joyful, when you attain that state of being. Joy as an emotion is the one that most people want to increase.

I'm not talking about being happy, I'm talking about being in a joyful state. Happy is enjoying or characterized by well-being and contentment, expressing, reflecting, or suggestive of, having or marked by an atmosphere of good fellowship.

Joy is the emotion evoked by well-being, success, or good fortune or by the prospect of possessing what one desires, the expression or exhibition of such emotion, a state of happiness or felicity, a source or cause of delight.

Joy as a choice; it seems like an easy initiative. I told myself to be happy, when I had a bad day, I rose the next day and told myself to be happy. And I did that day after day, never understanding why I kept feeling negatively. Starting to see the insanity? **Simply making the statements to myself without an intelligent plan of action meant that I was never going to achieve my goal.**

The Joy Codex is that action plan, intelligent application of specific elements with built in measurement and reinforcement in order to achieve a purpose, a joyful state.

Joyful is happiness with intelligent cognitive intention and cognitive understanding. You have implemented the previous four elements of compassion, integrity, and responsibility and now you are ready for joy.

As you may recall, thought →emotion →behavior.

People often convey to me that they are happy. The thing about being a joyful person, that joy radiates from within for the world to see. **The type of statements you make about self and others, and your actions determine if you are a joyful person.**

These people tell me they are happy, however when they communicate, they communicate with negativity. They will say "I'm only bitching," or "I'm only communicating." **Bitching and complaining is a behavior that stems from negative thoughts that led to negative emotions about self and others.** This behavior is not congruent with a joyful state. I've made that statement a few times, it's important.

When you think negative thoughts about yourself and others, you aren't in a joyful state. When you speak to yourself and others with resentment, disdain, contempt, rudeness, anger, hatred, or apathy you aren't in a joyful state. When you drink alcohol every day or take mind-altering substances you aren't in a joyful state. Remember the goal is to increase joy, negativity decreases joy.

I'm able to quickly identify a person that isn't in a joyful state based on their behavior. Acting happy and saying nice things to other people doesn't make that individual a joyful person. Being successful at the transactional things, which includes rote statements to others about your happiness in life, may induce some happiness and a sense of accomplishment. It isn't enough to increase joy, **joyful is a state of being not a transaction**.

The way you communicate represents your state of being, in order to speak it, you must think it, which leads to feeling it and then behaving in that manner.

Earlier in the book we determined that there are three types of people, unhappy, neutral, and joyful. Go back and reread that section on the three types of people if you don't recall these types. Joyful individuals are always looking for solutions to improve, making the choice, creating an action plan, and taking the steps for that improvement.

Being positive and solution oriented goes a long way in our society, especially when it comes to personal and professional relationships. I prefer people that are joyful. I want joyful individuals on my team, to work for me, to be my friends, to be associates, and I also want to have acquaintances that are joyful. I want joyful people in my life and again, I'm talking about a joyful person, not someone who tells you how happy they are.

It's really a pleasure for me when I interact with people that are accountable for their joyful state.

It feels great to act with the elements of The Joy Codex (TJC), when exemplify compassion, I feel joy, when I elevate integrity, I feel joy, when I demonstrate cognitive responsibility, I feel joy, when I operate with and have cognitive clarity, I feel joy; and when I intentionally choose joy, I sustain joy.

I've made the personal and intimate connection with behavior and my state of being. You are doing the same when you connect each of your actions to specific thoughts and emotions. That takes awareness and skill; you have the skillset.

When I arise each day, prior to even getting out of bed, I mentally say to myself, "**I CHOOSE JOY TOAY!**" Just like that, all caps and bold. I want to make sure that **I hear** what I'm laying down, because my day depends on hearing that message. I'm making choices when I start each day, I want to exemplify compassion, elevate integrity, demonstrate responsibility, operate with clarity and choose joy for self and others; it's that simple.

Make the choice to improve your affect through an intelligent plan. It helps to know what things increase your joy. Do you know what brings you joy? When you experience a joyous moment, do you identify the cause? When your behavior is negative, do you change your thoughts from negative to positive? Are you in control? Do you want to feel better emotionally? Choose joy and the actions that increase that joyful state.

The Joy Codex is a holistic methodology, making the statement of "I choose joy" isn't enough to make the jump to a joyful state. **A holistically joyful state includes compassion, integrity, responsibility, clarity, and joy applied to self and others consistently**. There is a deep interconnection between the elements and a joyful state. You improve with a joyful state.

Barriers to Success

Not understanding or implementing all the components and elements of The Joy Codex as recommended is a barrier to success. Ensure that your goal each day is to act (behavior) with the foundational principles of The Joy Codex. If you're unsure of a word or concept, ask someone or use google. At this point in the book, you are clear on what each element entails and have implemented the worksheets as recommended.

Negative people are a barrier to your success, they make excuses for their unhappiness and refuse to focus on solutions that improve their outcomes. Remember that being sympathetic or empathetic doesn't mean that you should get drawn into their emotional state. You may exemplify compassion for them without accepting their state of being as your own.

I'm certain that you are already thinking about boundary setting in these circumstances. When another has the ability to become more enlightened and chooses misery, unhappiness, and a negative disposition, boundary setting is the best course of action for you.

Surround yourself with people that have the same positive outlook and determination that you have incorporated into your life. Joy is something you want, and you've done the work, put in the effort, the time, the emotion, and the thought; all to increase your joy.

Expecting others around you to create and sustain your joy is also a barrier to you achieving true sustainable joy. There are so many reasons why this is a major pitfall.

Only you can implement the changes, make the choice to invest in your well-being. What do you want? Will you go to any length to get what you want? **I wanted secular spiritual homeostasis and increased my joy holistically through a deep commitment to compassion, integrity, responsibility, and clarity for self and others.**

Falling back into old patterns, negative ways of thinking, negative communication styles, and apathy about self and others is still expected, however at this point in The Joy Codex Method, I expect you to identify those moments and correct them. You have the skillset and tools to rectify all negative thought, emotion, and behavior. Joy is a choice. Remember at the begging of the book that 40% of your joy is a choice.

When I'm feeling emotionally sad, the first things I do is determine if my thoughts are the cause, if my thoughts are the cause, then I change my thoughts.

When I'm having a difficult time communicating with another individual and I'm being snarky, sarcastic, impatient, or feeling resentful, I take a moment (minding the gap) and determine if my thoughts are in line with my desire to increase joy and attain a joyful state of being.

Dealing with others that are using/abusing alcohol and mind-altering substances are a challenge, **they have lost their ability to regulate thought and therefore they are unable to regulate emotion and behavior**. Boundaries work best for your success.

Final Thoughts

When I choose joy, I improve. **Knowing I want to increase joy for myself, I'm always comparing my behavior and emotions to my thoughts, making a clear choice to incorporate corrections (improvements) to achieve the**

outcome; increasing joy. Joy is a choice, make the choice to increase joy by incorporating the components you have implemented; compassion, integrity, responsibility, clarity, and now joy. Use your measurements of success to improve your outcomes. In order to choose joy, you are cognitive of how your thoughts influence your emotions and behaviors; making improvements to your mood. Awareness of joyful moments and what led to those joyful moments is key to your success. When you are joyful, trace that back to what you did to achieve that success.

Spend the next seven days focusing on your commitment to joy as you complete the joy worksheets each day. Be vigilant in your actions, knowing what will increase joy, know when those things happen and allow yourself to enjoy your success.

Complete honesty when answering the worksheets will increase your joy. A score achieved through dishonesty only serves to exacerbate your misery, your goal is to increase joy. When you know what your score is from day to day, you have the ability to make changes that will increase your joy the following day.

It's time to put what you've learned into action! Now you get to see the results. Know that you are making intelligent choices combined with intention and action.

Worksheets

In order to implement The Joy Codex Methodology, you will need to utilize the following forms. Continuation of the new behavior requires reinforcement; the forms below will provide everything you need. Complete each of the worksheets for the duration listed below using the instructions provided.

Print enough copies of each worksheet based on the instructions below. For best results follow the directions exactly.

At the end of the book, there are additional worksheets that may be of value to you today. Please review these worksheets and determine if they are applicable for that moment. The worksheets are the "SOaR Monthly," "What Element Could I Have Applied," "Change My Thoughts,

Emotions, Behaviors" "Thoughts, Emotions, Behaviors," and "The Behavior I want, via, Thought and Emotion."

The Joy Codex Survey Joy (Days 1 and Day 7) 2 copies.

THE JOY CODEX SURVEY				JOY			

Name: Date: TJC Rank:

	Pick one answer per question that best describes your current feelings about joy.	ANSWER				Score	Weight	Total
1	Do you know what joyousness feels like?	Y	S	N	NS		1	
2	How often do you deeply experience joy?**	D	W	M	Q		3	
3	Are you aware of those joyous moments?	Y	S	N	NS		2	
4	Are you aware of the things you do that increase your joy?	Y	S	N	NS		2	
5	Do you create moments that increase your Joy?	Y	S	N	NS		3	
6	Do you represent joy to Self and Others?	Y	S	N	NS		3	
7	Do you feel joy for Others when they experience joy?	Y	S	N	NS		4	
8	Do you create situations to increase joy for Others?	Y	S	N	NS		4	
9	Do you start each day with the intention of increasing joy?	Y	S	N	NS		5	
10	Do you want more joy in your life?	Y	S	N	NS		4	
11	Do you have the skill and tools to increase joy in your life?	Y	S	N	NS		5	
12	Are you willing to dedicate your time and energy to increasing your joy?	Y	S	N	NS		5	

KEY Y=YES, S=SOMETIMES, N=NEVER, NS=NOT SURE

Sum Total:
Sum Total /10:
New Total*2:

Round Totals Up or Down to Nearest Decimal

Key Score		Measurement Rules	Rankings
Y	6	In order to get the TJC Rank, multiply the Score column by the Weight column for each question.	47-50 Joyful +
N	1	Enter that number in the Total column. Add the Total column and enter that number in to the Sum Total field.	42-46 Joyful
SOMETIMES	3	Divide the number in the Sum Total field by 10 and rounding up or down to the nearest decimal. Enter that	36-41 Joyful -
NOT SURE	2	number in the Sum Total / 10 field. Multiply the Sum Total / 10 field by 2, rounding up or down to nearest decimal.	31-35 Neutral +
		Enter that number in the New Total*2 field. Compare that number to the Rankings and enter your ranking	24-30 Neutral
		in the TJC Rank field at the top of the form. As an example, if I scored 39, I would write out Joyful-	16-23 Neutral -
			≤ 15 Unhappy

BWWJY001.3   www.thejoycodex.com   Codex Capstone Media L.L.C.

Take the Joy Codex Survey on days 1 and 7. You may take the survey all 7 days to get an extra little bit of boost as you start each day. The survey is a gage for you to understand your current feelings about joy and will get you grounded in the new element you have just learned about. The measurement on the worksheet is a benchmark for you to increase your results based on your answers. You will know which areas to improve upon for the next day, you will be more focused.

The Joy Codex Elements In Action Joy (Days 1-7) 1 copy used throughout the 7 days.

The Joy Codex Elements In Action — Joy		
Choose Joy	**Choose Unhappiness**	
1	Knowing that joy is a state of being and a cognitive choice.	1	Knowing that joy is a state of being and acting incongruent to increasing joy.
2	Measuring your progress in order to make improvements.	2	Not clear cognitively, no plan in place to measure progress.
3	Communicating with the intention of **increasing joy** for Self and Others.	3	Communicating with the intention of **increasing unhappiness** for all.
4	Knowing your thoughts about Self and Others, determines if you are joyful.	4	Disregard for thoughts leading to negative emotion, and behavior.
5	Actions that are in alignment with a joyful state of being.	5	Actions that aren't in alignment with a joyful state of being.
6	Having an action plan with the intention of improving your well-being.	6	Lack of an action plan, lack of implementing an action plan.
7	Being accountable for increasing joy for Self and Others.	7	No accountability to increase joy for Self and Others.
8		8	
9		9	
10		10	
11		11	
12		12	
13		13	
14		14	
15		15	
16		16	

Use the spaces provided to add the items you have identified showing you operate w/ clarity and the items that don't. How do your thoughts influence your clarity with regard to self and others? How will you operate w/ clarity and what is the opposite of your action item, how will you know when it isn't demonstrated?

BWWJY005.0   www.thejoycodex.com   Codex Capstone Media L.L.C.©

The Joy Codex Elements In Action worksheet challenges you to put your knowledge into action and to be cognitively aware when your actions are incongruent with The Joy Codex.

The Joy Codex Inventory Joy (Days 1-7) 1 copy used throughout the 7 days.

The Joy Codex Inventory Joy

List the things you will do to chose joy for Self and Others.

Self	Others
1	1
2	2
3	3
4	4
5	5
6	6
7	7
8	8
9	9
10	10
11	11
12	12
13	13
14	14
15	15
16	16
17	17
18	18
19	19
20	20

BWWJY0004.0   www.thejoycodex.com   Codex Capstone Media L.L.C.

The Joy Codex Inventory is a list of the items/people/places/things that you do that demonstrate what you do for self and others within the given element.

The Joy Codex Quick Start Joy (Days 1-7, at the start of your day) 7 copies.

THE JOY CODEX QUICK START			JOY			

Name: _____ Date: _____ TJC Rank: _____

	Pick one answer per question that best describes your action plan for success today.	ANSWER	Score	Weight	Total
1	I know what TJC joy entails for Self and Others today.	Y S N NS		5	
2	I will choose joy for Self and Others today.	Y S N NS		4	
3	I will have patience with Self and Others today.	Y S N NS		3	
4	I will be kind to Self and Others today.	Y S N NS		3	
5	I will think positively about Self and Others today.	Y S N NS		3	
6	I will take a moment to engage in an activity that increases my joy today.	Y S N NS		3	
7	I will share my joyful disposition with others today.	Y S N NS		4	
8	When I experience joy for Self and Others today, I will be aware of that emotion.	Y S N NS		4	
9	I will identify the interactions that increase my joy for Self and Others today.	Y S N NS		5	
10	I will complete the Quick Wrap Joy today.	Y S N NS		4	
11	I will complete the SOaR worksheet today.	Y S N NS		5	

Sum Total: _____

KEY Y=YES, S=SOMETIMES, N=NEVER, NS=NOT SURE

Sum Total /10: _____

New Total*2: _____

Round Totals Up or Down to Nearest Decimal

Key Score		Measurement Rules	Rankings
Y	6	In order to get the TJC Rank, multiply the Score column by the Weight column for each question.	49-52 Joyful +
N	1	Enter that number in the Total column. Add the Total column and enter that number in to the Sum Total field.	44-48 Joyful
SOMETIMES	3	Divide the number in the Sum Total field by 10 and rounding up or down to the nearest decimal. Enter that	39-43 Joyful -
NOT SURE	2	number in the Sum Total / 10 field. Multiply the Sum Total / 10 field by 2, rounding up or down to nearest decimal	33-38 Neutral +
		Enter that number in the New Total*2 field. Compare that number to the Rankings and enter your ranking	27-32 Neutral
		in the TJC Rank field at the top of the form. As an example, if I scored 39, I would write out Joyful-	16-26 Neutral -
			≤ 15 Unhappy

BWWJY002.1   www.thejoycodex.com   Codex Capstone Media L.L.C.©

The Joy Codex Quick Start is an antecedent, the worksheet will prompt you at the start of your day to focus on specific points within the worksheet based on the unique element you are working on. This will be completed the start of each day. The Quick Start worksheet has specific "I" statements to prepare your brain for success that day. The measurement on the form is a benchmark for you to increase your results based on your answers. You will know which areas to improve upon for the next day, you will be more focused.

The Joy Codex Quick Wrap Joy (Days 1-7 at the end of your day) 7 copies.

	THE JOY CODEX QUICK WRAP	JOY				
Name: Date: TJC Rank:						

	Pick one answer per question that best describes your success for today.	ANSWER				Score	Weight	Total
1	Today I knew what joy meant for Self and Others.	Y	S	N	NS		5	
2	Today I chose joy for Self and Others.	Y	S	N	NS		4	
3	Today I improved my state of being.	Y	S	N	NS		3	
4	Today I made the choice to mind the gap and increase joy.	Y	S	N	NS		3	
5	Today I incorporated the elements of compassion, integrity, responsibility, clarity, and joy for Self and Others.	Y	S	N	NS		3	
6	Today I was aware of those moments that I chose joy for Self and Others.	Y	S	N	NS		3	
7	Today I communicated with the intention if increasing joy for Self and Others.	Y	S	N	NS		4	
8	Today I shared my joy.	Y	S	N	NS		4	
9	Today I identified the interactions that increased joy Self and Others.	Y	S	N	NS		5	
10	Today I Completed the Quick Wrap Joy worksheet.	Y	S	N	NS		4	
11	Today I completed the SOaR worksheet.	Y	S	N	NS		5	

KEY Y=YES, S=SOMETIMES, N=NEVER, NS=NOT SURE

Sum Total:
Sum Total /10:
New Total*2:

Round Totals Up or Down to Nearest Decimal

Key Score		Measurement Rules	Rankings
Y	6	In order to get the TJC Rank, multiply the Score column by the Weight column for each question.	49-52 Joyful +
N	1	Enter that number in the Total column. Add the Total column and enter that number in to the Sum Total field.	44-48 Joyful
SOMETIMES	3	Divide the number in the Sum Total field by 10 and rounding up or down to the nearest decimal. Enter that	39-43 Joyful -
NOT SURE	2	number in the Sum Total / 10 field. Multiply the Sum Total / 10 field by 2, rounding up or down to nearest decimal.	33-38 Neutral +
		Enter that number in the New Total*2 field. Compare that number to the Rankings and enter your ranking	26-32 Neutral
		in the TJC Rank field at the top of the form. As an example, if I scored 39, I would write out Joyful-	16-26 Neutral -
			≤ 15 Unhappy

BWWJY003.0   www.thejoycodex.com   Codex Capstone Media L.L.C.©

The Joy Codex Quick Wrap worksheet is a review of your day specific to the element you are implementing. The questions are designed to stimulate your thought process about your day specific to each question and your application of the component. There is an expectation that you will review your day mentally and answer the questions thoughtfully. The measurement on the worksheet is a benchmark for you to increase your results based on your answers. You will know which areas to improve upon for the next day.

The Joy Codex SOaR Daily Log (Day 1-7 at the end of your day) 7 copies.

The Joy Codex SOaR Daily Log

Date	Rank (circle one icon that represents your day)	Score

Today I had a _____ day because _____
TJC RANK   the reasons you ranked Unhappy or Neutral or Joyful

Tomorrow I will _____
                detail the actions you will take to increase your success

TJC Rank
5 Unhappy
10 Neutral
15 Joyful

5   10   15
          Key Score

Name: _____
Rank: _____

BWWBR001.0   www.thejoycodex.com   Codex Capstone Media L.L.C.

The Joy Codex SOaR Daily Log is a schedule of reinforcement. The form is very simple to use, there are three icons, you will select the one that best represents how your day went in relation to applying the new skills and tools you are learning. From left to right the icons represent a day that required charging as you were unable to implement the element as desired. The middle icon represents a day that didn't go 100% as planned. You started your day with the Quick Start worksheet, you were cognizant of the specific items within each element, however, you found yourself slipping back into old behavior. The icon on the right is the full charge battery, this is a great day. You were completely aware of the Quick Start items that day and knew when you implemented them. The worksheet also has two statements from you; what the specific reasons were for your ranking that day, and a statement about what you will do specifically the next day to improve and succeed. The measurement on the worksheet is a benchmark for you to increase your results based on your answers. You will know which areas to improve upon for the next day, you will be more focused.

19 THE JOY CODEX ALL ELEMENTS

Now it's time to bring all the elements together.

ICODEX CYPHER			
Ownership	**Action**	**Characteristic**	**Personalization**
When I	eXemplify	Compassion	I Feel
When I	Elevate	Integrity	I Know
When I	Demonstrate	Responsibility	I Act
When I	Operate with	Clarity	I Measure
When I	Choose	Joy	I Improve
When I	Implement	The Joy Codex	I Succeed

BWWFAL004.0   www.thejoycodex.com   Codex Capstone Media L.L.C©

Refresher

Compassion is a sympathetic or empathetic consciousness of other's or self's' distress, together with a desire to mitigate or alleviate it.

Exemplify as an action word means to show or lead by example. Exemplifying compassion is showing positive feelings and emotions for self and others, leading by example. When I exemplify compassion for self and others; I feel.

Integrity is an adherence to a code especially moral or artistic values, an unimpaired condition, and the quality or state of being complete or undivided.

Elevate as an action word means to lift-up, raise in rank, to improve morally, culturally, and intellectually. Elevating integrity is knowing that you act ethically, morally, and with values every time. When I elevate integrity; I know.

Responsibility is a quality or state of being responsible (moral, legal, or mental accountability), reliable, trustworthy, something for which one is responsible.

Demonstrate as an action word means to show clearly, to make clear by reasoning or evidence, and to show value. Demonstrating responsibility encompasses knowing that compassion and integrity are key drivers in achieving joy and self-actualization and being accountable to acting with purpose. When I demonstrate responsibility, I act.

Clarity is the quality or state of being clear, coherent, intelligible and transparent.

Operate as an action word means to perform a function, to produce an appropriate effect, and to perform a series of functions. When operating with clarity you are acting intelligently, behaving with the intention to achieve a purpose, you measure your results to determine effectiveness and make changes. When I operate with clarity, I measure.

Joy is an emotional state that is characterized by feelings of elation, euphoria, ecstasy, delight, happiness, jubilation, gratification, pleasure, satisfaction, and well-being.

Choose as an action word means to select after consideration, to decide, to plan and to have a preference. Choose joy encompasses a decision, a plan, and after careful consideration, implementation with the intention to improve and increase feelings of joy. When I choose joy, I improve.

Everything I do to self; I do to others. Everything I do to others; I do to self. They are intimately connected. Actions for and about self, have an influence on interactions with others. Behavior for and about another, impacts self.

You've also learned that your thoughts help regulate your emotions and behavior. Change your thoughts, change the world.

You must know what you want, you must have an action plan, measurement, and reinforcement in order to affectively change and improve.

The next seven days will assess your cognitive understanding and implementation of The Joy Codex. If you begin to fall back into old patterns, determine where the break-down is and make the changes required to succeed.

How you think, speak, and act are all indicators of your success. You started this journey to experience life more joyfully, take the steps necessary to succeed. You are competent and application of The Joy Codex on a daily basis as directed will increase your joy.

Barriers to Success

An overabundance of confidence and apathy are barriers to success. It's important to complete the last group of worksheets, so that you may implement The Joy Codex in its entirety and reinforce that new behavior. Awareness of how you are thinking and feeling, will keep you aligned with your values and principals.

Final Thoughts

When I implement The Joy Codex, I succeed. Consistent application of The Joy Codex will provide a dependable increase in joy. Your goal to increase joy has been a journey, and you've put a great deal of effort into succeeding.

Remember, negative thoughts are also precursors to negative emotions, like sadness, anger, and anxiety. The more you dwell on negative thoughts, the more deep-rooted they become. Ruminating on negative thoughts, even ones as simple as the word no, physically impact your brain structure, making you more prone to negative thoughts in the future. Negative thoughts decrease joy and lead to unintended behavior. Replace your inner dialogue with positivity.

Spend the next seven days focusing on implementing the elements of The Joy Codex, exemplify compassion, elevate integrity, demonstrate responsibility, operate with clarity, and choose joy. Be vigilant knowing what will increase joy, know when those things happen and allow yourself to succeed.

Complete honesty when answering the worksheets will help you succeed. Your goal is to increase joy by implementing all of the elements this week. When you know what your score is from day to day, you have the ability to make changes that will increase your joy the following day.

It's time to put what you've learned into action! Know that you are making intelligent choices combined with intention and action all with the purpose if increasing joy.

Worksheets

In order to implement The Joy Codex Methodology, you will need to utilize the following forms. Continuation of the new behavior requires reinforcement; the forms below will provide everything you need. Complete each of the worksheets for the duration listed below using the instructions provided.

Print enough copies of each worksheet based on the instructions below. For best results follow the directions exactly.

At the end of the book, there are additional worksheets that may be of value to you today. Please review these worksheets and determine if they are applicable for that moment. The worksheets are the "SOaR Monthly," "What Element Could I Have Applied," "Change My Thoughts, Emotions, Behaviors" "Thoughts, Emotions, Behaviors," and "The Behavior I want, via, Thought and Emotion."

The Joy Codex Survey All Elements (Days 1 and Day 7) 2 copies.

THE JOY CODEX SURVEY — ALL ELEMENTS

Name: _____ Date: _____ TJC Rank: _____

#	Pick one answer per question that best describes your current feelings about responsibility.	ANSWER							Score	Weight	Total
1	Do you know what all of the elements of TJC entails for Self and Others?	Y	S	N	NS					3	
2	How often do you act with all of the elements of TJC?**	D	W	M	Q	A	N	NS		3	
3	Are you aware of those moments that you act with the principles of TJC for Self and Others?	Y	S	N	NS					2	
4	Does your behavior reflect TJC principles for Self?	Y	S	N	NS					2	
5	Do you demonstrate TJC principles?	Y	S	N	NS					3	
6	Do you set healthy boundaries with TJC as a primary influence?	Y	S	N	NS					3	
7	Do you act cognitively with the principles of TJC when interacting with Others?	Y	S	N	NS					4	
8	Do you communicate with the principles of TJC ?	Y	S	N	NS					4	
9	Do you start each day with the intention to demonstrate TJC for Self and Others?	Y	S	N	NS					5	
10	Do you want to act cognitively with TJC for Self and Others?	Y	S	N	NS					4	
11	Do you have the skill and tools to implement the principles of The Joy Codex in your life?	Y	S	N	NS					5	
12	Are you willing to dedicate your time and energy to implementing The Joy Codex?	Y	S	N	NS					5	

Sum Total:

KEY Y=YES, S=SOMETIMES, N=NEVER, NS=NOT SURE

Sum Total /10:

DAILY/WEEKLY/MONTHLY/QUARTERLY/ANNUALLY/NEVER /NOT SURE (pick one)

New Total*2:

Round Totals Up or Down to Nearest Decimal

Key Score		Measurement Rules	Rankings
Y	6		49-52 Joyful +
N	1	In order to get the TJC Rank, multiply the Score column by the Weight column for each question.	44-48 Joyful
SOMETIMES	3	Enter that number in the Total column. Add the Total column and enter that number in to the Sum Total field.	39-43 Joyful -
NOT SURE	2	Divide the number in the Sum Total field by 10 and rounding up or down to the nearest decimal. Enter that	33-38 Neutral +
DAILY	6	number in the Sum Total / 10 field. Multiply the Sum Total / 10 field by 2, rounding up or down to nearest decimal.	27-32 Neutral
WEEKLY	5	Enter that number in the New Total*2 field. Compare that number to the Rankings and enter your ranking	16-26 Neutral -
MONTHLY	4	in the TJC Rank field at the top of the form. As an example, if I scored 39, I would write out Joyful-	≤ 15 Unhappy
QUARTERLY	3		
ANNUALLY	2		
NEVER	1		

BWWAL006.0   www.thejoycodex.com   Codex Capstone Media L.L.C.©

Take the Joy Codex Survey on days 1 and 7. You may take the survey all 7 days to get an extra little bit of boost as you start each day. The survey is a gage for you to understand your current feelings about all of the elements and will get you grounded on The Joy Codex. The measurement on the worksheet is a benchmark for you to increase your results based on your answers. You will know which areas to improve upon for the next day, you will be more focused.

The Joy Codex Elements In Action All Elements (Days 1-7) 1 copy used throughout the 7 days.

	The Joy Codex Elements In Action Implement The Joy Codex		ALL ELEMENTS No Action Plan For Improvement
1	Acting with compassion, integrity, responsibility, clarity, and joy.	1	Acting without compassion, integrity, responsibility, clarity, and joy.
2	Engagement in activities that are congruent with The Joy Codex.	2	Engagement in activities that are incongruent to The joy Codex.
3	Act with intention, implementing The Joy Codex.	3	Actions without intention for improvement.
4	Communicating with the principles of The Joy Codex.	4	Communicating without the principles of The Joy Codex, decreasing well-being.
5	Minding the gap with all elements in order to RESPOND rather than react.	5	Immediately REACTING without awareness.
6	Treating Self and Others with compassion, integrity, responsibility, clarity, and joy.	6	Treating Self and Others without concern for well-being.
7	Making choices today that will positively impact your life each and every day.	7	Making poor choices that increase pain, suffering, and unhappiness.
8		8	
9		9	
10		10	
11		11	
12		12	
13		13	
14		14	
15		15	
16		16	

Use the spaces provided to add the items you have identified that demonstrate The Joy Codex in action and the items that don't. How do your thoughts influence your behavior regard to implementing The Joy Codex? How will you implement all of the elements and what is the opposite of your action item, how will you know when it isn't demonstrated?

BWWAL005.2   www.thejoycodex.com   Codex Capstone Media L.L.C.©

The Joy Codex Elements In Action worksheet challenges you to put your knowledge into action and to be cognitively aware when your actions are incongruent with The Joy Codex.

The Joy Codex Inventory All Elements (Days 1-7) 1 copy used throughout the 7 days.

The Joy Codex Inventory All

List the things you will do to incorporate all charachteristics for Self and Others.

Self	Others
1	1
2	2
3	3
4	4
5	5
6	6
7	7
8	8
9	9
10	10
11	11
12	12
13	13
14	14
15	15
16	16
17	17
18	18
19	19
20	20

BWWAL0004.0   www.thejoycodex.com   Codex Capstone Media L.L.C.

The Joy Codex Inventory is a list of the items/people/places/things that you do that demonstrate what you do for self and others within the given element.

The Joy Codex Quick Start All Elements (Days 1-7, at the start of your day) 7 copies.

	THE JOY CODEX QUICK START ALL ELEMENTS							
	Name: Date: TJC Rank:					Score	Weight	Total
	Pick one answer per question that best describes your action plan for success today.		ANSWER					
1	I deeply understand each element of the Joy Codex today.	Y	S	N	NS		5	
2	I will implement the elements of The Joy Codex for Self and Others today.	Y	S	N	NS		4	
3	I will be cognitively positive for Self and Others today.	Y	S	N	NS		3	
4	I will be communicate with the principles of The Joy Codex today.	Y	S	N	NS		3	
5	I will overcome any barriers to success today.	Y	S	N	NS		3	
6	I will measure my success today.	Y	S	N	NS		3	
7	I will respond to Others with the elements of The Joy Codex today.	Y	S	N	NS		4	
8	I will be cognitive of the impact that my thoughts have on my emotions which translates to my behavior.	Y	S	N	NS		4	
9	I will identify the interactions that increase compassion, integrity, responsibility, clarity, and joy for Self and Others today.	Y	S	N	NS		5	
10	I will complete the Quick Wrap All Elements worksheet today.	Y	S	N	NS		4	
11	I will complete the SOaR worksheet today.	Y	S	N	NS		5	

KEY Y=YES, S=SOMETIMES, N=NEVER, NS=NOT SURE

Sum Total:
Sum Total /10:
New Total*2:
Round Totals Up or Down to Nearest Decimal

Key Score		Measurement Rules	Rankings
Y	6	In order to get the TJC Rank, multiply the Score column by the Weight column for each question.	49-52 Joyful +
N	1	Enter that number in the Total column. Add the Total column and enter that number in to the Sum Total field.	44-48 Joyful
SOMETIMES	3	Divide the number in the Sum Total field by 10 and rounding up or down to the nearest decimal. Enter that	39-43 Joyful -
NOT SURE	2	number in the Sum Total / 10 field. Multiply the Sum Total / 10 field by 2 rounding up or down to nearest decimal.	33-38 Neutral +
		Enter that number in the New Total*2 field. Compare that number to the Rankings and enter your ranking	27-32 Neutral
		in the TJC Rank field at the top of the form. As an example, if I scored 39, I would write out Joyful-	16-26 Neutral -
			≤ 15 Unhappy

BWWAL002.2   www.thejoycodex.com   Codex Capstone Media L.L.C.©

The Joy Codex Quick Start is an antecedent, the worksheet will prompt you at the start of your day to focus on specific points within the worksheet based on the unique element you are working on. This will be completed at the start of each day. The Quick Start worksheet has specific "I" statements to prepare your brain for success that day. The measurement on the form is a benchmark for you to increase your results based on your answers. You will know which areas to improve upon for the next day, you will be more focused.

The Joy Codex Quick Wrap All Elements (Days 1-7 at the end of your day) 7 copies.

	THE JOY CODEX QUICK WRAP ALL ELEMENTS						

Name:_____ Date:_____ TJC Rank:_____

	Pick one answer per question that best describes your action plan for success today.	ANSWER				Score	Weight	Total
1	Today I deeply understood each element of the Joy Codex.	Y	S	N	NS		5	
2	Today I implemented the elements of The Joy Codex for Self and Others.	Y	S	N	NS		4	
3	Today I was cognitively positive for Self and Others.	Y	S	N	NS		3	
4	Today I communicated with the principles of The Joy Codex.	Y	S	N	NS		3	
5	Today I overcame any barriers to success.	Y	S	N	NS		3	
6	Today I measured my success throughout the day.	Y	S	N	NS		3	
7	Today I responded to Others with the elements of The Joy Codex in mind.	Y	S	N	NS		4	
8	Today I was cognitive of the impact that my thoughts had on my emotions which translated to my behavior.	Y	S	N	NS		4	
9	Today I identified the interactions that increase compassion, integrity, responsibility, clarity, and joy for Self and Others.	Y	S	N	NS		5	
10	Today I completed the Quick Wrap All Elements worksheet.	Y	S	N	NS		4	
11	Today I completed the SOaR worksheet.	Y	S	N	NS		5	

Sum Total:
Sum Total /10:
New Total*2:

KEY Y=YES, S=SOMETIMES, N=NEVER, NS=NOT SURE

Round Totals Up or Down to Nearest Decimal

Key Score		Measurement Rules	Rankings
Y	6	In order to get the TJC Rank, multiply the Score column by the Weight column for each question.	49-52 Joyful +
N	1	Enter that number in the Total column. Add the Total column and enter that number in to the Sum Total field.	44-48 Joyful
SOMETIMES	3	Divide the number in the Sum Total field by 10 and rounding up or down to the nearest decimal. Enter that	39-43 Joyful -
NOT SURE	2	number in the Sum Total / 10 field. Multiply the Sum Total / 10 field by 2 rounding up or down to nearest decimal.	33-38 Neutral +
		Enter that number in the New Total*2 field. Compare that number to the Rankings and enter your ranking	27-32 Neutral
		in the TJC Rank field at the top of the form. As an example, if I scored 39, I would write out Joyful-	16-26 Neutral -
			≤ 15 Unhappy

BWWAL003.0   www.thejoycodex.com   Codex Capstone Media L.L.C.©

The Joy Codex Quick Wrap worksheet is a review of your day specific to the element you are implementing. The questions are designed to stimulate your thought process about your day specific to each question and your application of the component. There is an expectation that you will review your day mentally and answer the questions thoughtfully. The measurement on the worksheet is a benchmark for you to increase your results based on your answers. You will know which areas to improve upon for the next day, you will be more focused.

The Joy Codex SOaR Daily Log (Day 1-7 at the end of your day) 7 copies.

The Joy Codex SOaR Daily Log is a schedule of reinforcement. The form is very simple to use, there are three icons, you will select the one that best represents how your day went in relation to applying the new skills and tools you are learning. From left to right the icons represent a day that required charging as you were unable to implement the element as desired. The middle icon represents a day that didn't go 100% as planned. You started your day with the Quick Start worksheet, you were cognizant of the specific items within each element, however, you found yourself slipping back into old behavior. The icon on the right is the full charge battery, this is a great day; you were cooking with gas or running on all cylinders. You were completely aware of the Quick Start items that day and knew when you implemented them. The worksheet also has two statements from you; what the specific reasons were for your ranking that day, and a statement about what you will do specifically the next day to improve and succeed. The measurement on the worksheet is a benchmark for you to increase your results based on your answers. You will know which areas to improve upon for the next day, you will be more focused.

20 BRINGING IT ALL TOGETHER

With The Joy Codex you are making the decision to implement a rigorous program of self-discovery through understanding, measurement, action, and reinforcement.

The Joy Codex ICODEX Cypher

The I in ICODEX has a dual meaning, "I" as in "me" and "I" as in "implement." I am the one acting and I have ownership of the elements, and finally I will implement what I know, measure, and succeed.

ICODEX CYPHER			
Ownership	**Action**	**Characteristic**	**Personalization**
When I	eXemplify	Compassion	I Feel
When I	Elevate	Integrity	I Know
When I	Demonstrate	Responsibility	I Act
When I	Operate with	Clarity	I Measure
When I	Choose	Joy	I Improve
When I	Implement	The Joy Codex	I Succeed
BWWFAL004.0	www.thejoycodex.com	Codex Capstone Media L.L.C©	

Print this ICODEX Cypher cheat sheet and apply to your monitor at work or home and the mirror you use to get ready each day. The ICODEX is an antecedent, prompting you to act within the context of TJC. This prompt will assist you in making positive choices for self and others.

Now that you've completed The Joy Codex and you fully comprehend the technique you will have increased your joy and begun to achieve **Secular Spiritual Homeostasis**; an observance of a spiritual philosophy without adherence to a religion to achieve stable equilibrium maintained by physiological processes.

Implementing new behavior takes repetition, build new neural pathways for the behavior you want through reinforcement.

You are on the way to a new life with increased joy. You now have the knowledge and the skill to live a life more realized and fulfilling.

Today, I continue to use the **SOaR Monthly Worksheet**. And if I'm having a difficult time, and I'm feeling unhappy, I use the maintenance worksheets specific to **"What Element Could I Have Applied," "Change My Thoughts, Emotions, Behaviors" "Thoughts, Emotions, Behaviors," and "The Behavior I want, via, Thought and Emotion."**

I also use the worksheets from the specific elements when I feel like I need a boost in any particular element. Follow the worksheet directions specific to your focus.

I also re-read the chapters on the elements when I find myself slipping back into old negative patterns that lead to negative behaviors.

My joyful state is mine to cultivate and nurture and yours is too! Remember that this is "your life," go out into the world and be joyful! You have what it takes to be successful and joyful.

Visit www.thejoycodex.com and find me on Twitter @codexjoy, Facebook https://www.facebook.com/thejoycodexbook, You Tube, and Instagram https://www.instagram.com/thejoycodex/

Additional Worksheets

The Joy Codex The Behavior I Want, Via Thought & Emotion.

The Behavior I Want, Via Thought & Emotion

Name: _____   Date: _____

SPECIFIC BEHAVIOR GOAL

SPECIFIC BEHAVIOR GOAL

WHY DO YOU WANT THIS CHANGE?

WHY DO YOU WANT THIS CHANGE?

WHAT EMOTIONS WILL INFLUENCE YOUR GOAL OF BEHAVIOR

WHAT EMOTIONS WILL INFLUENCE YOUR GOAL OF BEHAVIOR

WHAT THOUGHTS WILL INFLUENCE YOUR EMOTIONS?

WHAT THOUGHTS WILL INFLUENCE YOUR EMOTIONS?

COMPASSION/INTEGRITY/RESPONSIBILITY/CLARITY/JOY
CIRICLE THE ELEMENTS THAT YOU WILL UTILIZE TO ACHIEVE YOUR GOAL

HOW WILL YOU APPLY THE SELECTED ELEMENTS? WHY DID YOU SLECECT THEM?

HOW WILL YOU APPLY THE SELECTED ELEMENTS? WHY DID YOU SLECECT THEM?

HOW WILL KNOW WHEN YOU HAVE BEEN SUCCESSFUL?

WHAT REINFORCEMENT WILL YOU BUILD-IN WHEN YOU ARE SUCCESSFUL?

Use the Behavior I Want, Via thought & Emotion worksheet to target specific behaviors you want to increase. As an example, to increase the behavior of working out, I would change my thoughts and emotions to include positive statements leading to a change in behavior. Be very specific.

BWWBR0010.0   www.thejoycodex.com   Codex Capstone Media L.L.C.

EXAMPLE

The Behavior I Want, Via Thought & Emotion	**EXAMPLE**

Name: *Scot Gorman*   Date: **9/5/2019**

I want to increase by positive internal dialogue by changing the inner dialogue
SPECIFIC BEHAVIOR GOAL

reducing my cognitive distortions with specific statements.
SPECIFIC BEHAVIOR GOAL

Negative internal dialogue brings negative results, and positive internal dialogue brings positive results.
WHY DO YOU WANT THIS CHANGE?

I quite simply want to feel better more often.
WHY DO YOU WANT THIS CHANGE?

I want to increase feelings of confidence, appreciation, love, and well-being for self.
WHAT EMOTIONS WILL INFLUENCE YOUR GOAL OF BEHAVIOR

WHAT EMOTIONS WILL INFLUENCE YOUR GOAL OF BEHAVIOR

I will replace any automatic negative thoughts with positive thoughts for self. I know that
WHAT THOUGHTS WILL INFLUENCE YOUR EMOTIONS?

I am just right and that my skills are equal to or comparable to my peers.
WHAT THOUGHTS WILL INFLUENCE YOUR EMOTIONS?

COMPASSION/*INTEGRITY*/RESPONSIBILITY/*CLARITY*/JOY
CIRICLE THE ELEMENTS THAT YOU WILL UTILIZE TO ACHIEVE YOUR GOAL

When I have a negative automatic thought, I will remember my integrity, thinking thoughts in-line
HOW WILL YOU APPLY THE SELECTED ELEMENTS? WHY DID YOU SLECECT THEM?

with my beliefs, values, ethics . And with clarity, I am clear that my thoughts influence my behavior.
HOW WILL YOU APPLY THE SELECTED ELEMENTS? WHY DID YOU SLECECT THEM?

When I change my thoughts and increase my joy I will know I accomplished my goal.
HOW WILL KNOW WHEN YOU HAVE BEEN SUCCESSFUL?

When I increase positive internal dialogue and feel joyful, I will be aware and make a mental note.
WHAT REINFORCEMENT WILL YOU BUILD-IN WHEN YOU ARE SUCCESSFUL?

Use the Behavior I Want, Via thought & Emotion worksheet to target specific behaviors you want to increase. As an example, to increase the behavior of working out, I would change my thoughts and emotions to include positive statements leading to a change in behavior. Be very specific.

BWWBR0010.0   www.thejoycodex.com   Codex Capstone Media L.L.C.

The Joy Codex SOaR Monthly Worksheet, print 1 copy.

The Joy Codex Monthly SOaR Worksheet											
Month Rank	Month Rank	Month Rank	Month Rank	Month Rank	Month Rank	Month Rank	Month Rank	Month Rank	Month Rank	Month Rank	Month Rank
Jan	Feb	Mar	Apr	Jun	Jul	Aug	Sep	Oct	Nov	Dec	
Jan Score	Feb Score	Mar Score	Apr Score	Jun Score	Jul Score	Aug Score	Sep Score	Oct Score	Nov Score	Dec Score	
1	1	1	1	1	1	1	1	1	1	1	
2	2	2	2	2	2	2	2	2	2	2	
3	3	3	3	3	3	3	3	3	3	3	
4	4	4	4	4	4	4	4	4	4	4	
5	5	5	5	5	5	5	5	5	5	5	
6	6	6	6	6	6	6	6	6	6	6	
7	7	7	7	7	7	7	7	7	7	7	
8	8	8	8	8	8	8	8	8	8	8	
9	9	9	9	9	9	9	9	9	9	9	
10	10	10	10	10	10	10	10	10	10	10	
11	11	11	11	11	11	11	11	11	11	11	
12	12	12	12	12	12	12	12	12	12	12	
13	13	13	13	13	13	13	13	13	13	13	
14	14	14	14	14	14	14	14	14	14	14	
15	15	15	15	15	15	15	15	15	15	15	
16	16	16	16	16	16	16	16	16	16	16	
17	17	17	17	17	17	17	17	17	17	17	
18	18	18	18	18	18	18	18	18	18	18	
19	19	19	19	19	19	19	19	19	19	19	
20	20	20	20	20	20	20	20	20	20	20	
21	21	21	21	21	21	21	21	21	21	21	
22	22	22	22	22	22	22	22	22	22	22	
23	23	23	23	23	23	23	23	23	23	23	
24	24	24	24	24	24	24	24	24	24	24	
25	25	25	25	25	25	25	25	25	25	25	
26	26	26	26	26	26	26	26	26	26	26	
27	27	27	27	27	27	27	27	27	27	27	
28	28	28	28	28	28	28	28	28	28	28	
29	29	29	29	29	29	29	29	29	29	29	
30	30	30	30	30	30	30	30	30	30	30	
31		31		31	31	31			31		31	

Score Key		Rank			Measurement	
TJC +/- equal to 15	TJC +	Joyful	Score 12-15		Add up the total months score and divide by the number of entries for the given month. Example, if I entered a score for each day in	
TJC ↔ is equal to 10	TJC ↔	Neutral	Score 8-11		January, that would be a total of 31 entries. Divide the total score by 31 days. That will provide you with a rank, enter the rank on the	
TJC - is equal to 5	TJC -	Unhappy	Score 0-7		top of the worksheet.	

The Joy Codex SOaR Monthly Worksheet is quick and easy to use and is a way for you to measure your daily, monthly, and yearly success. For each day of the month, you will determine if your score is TJC +, TJC ↔, TJC - based on your application of TJC method for that day.

The Joy Codex What Element Could I have Applied?
Worksheet

What Element Could I Have Applied?		
Name:		Date:
Today, I felt		when
	EMOTION	I or OTHERS NAME
did or didn't		
	ISSUE	
	ISSUE CONTINUED	
	ISSUE CONTINUED	
I Felt		because I thought
	EMOTION	WHAT WOULD HAPPEN
	WHAT WOULD HAPPEN CONTINUED	
	WHAT WOULD HAPPEN CONTINUED	
I will apply		
	TJC ELEMENT or TJC ELEMENTS	
with a focus on		
	SPECIFIC ITEMS RELEATED TO THOUGHTS, EMOTIONS, AND BEHAVIOR	
	SPECIFIC ITEMS CONTINUED THOUGHTS, EMOTIONS, AND BEHAVIOR	
	SPECIFIC ITEMS CONTINUED THOUGHTS, EMOTIONS, AND BEHAVIOR	
knowing that		
	TJC ELEMENT or TJC ELEMENTS	

applied to the situation and/or issue will increase joy by acting differently next time with

cognitive intention. I am committed to applying the element(s) above next-time the issue arises.

I'm responsible for my behavior and how it relates to The Joy Codex and increasing joy.

Use this worksheet when you're not sure which elements to apply to a situation or issue or had a bad interaction.

EXAMPLE

What Element Could I Have Applied?		**EXAMPLE**

Name: _Scot Gorman_   Date: _10/10/2019_

Today, I felt   _threatened_   when   _Joe (my boss)_
          EMOTION   I or OTHERS NAME

did or didn't   _started talking about off shoring many of my duties._
      ISSUE

      ISSUE CONTINUED

      ISSUE CONTINUED

I Felt   _threatened_   because I thought   _that my job was in_
          EMOTION   WHAT WOULD HAPPEN

          jeopardy.
     WHAT WOULD HAPPEN CONTINUED

      WHAT WOULD HAPPEN CONTINUED

I will apply   _CLARITY_
     TJC ELEMENT or TJC ELEMENTS

with a focus on   _knowing that I do a great job and that I could've asked my boss what would_
     SPECIFIC ITEMS RELEATED TO THOUGHTS, EMOTIONS, AND BEHAVIOR

      happen to my position if my functions were being off shored.
     SPECIFIC ITEMS CONTINUED THOUGHTS, EMOTIONS, AND BEHAVIOR

     SPECIFIC ITEMS CONTINUED THOUGHTS, EMOTIONS, AND BEHAVIOR

knowing that   _CLARITY_
     TJC ELEMENT or TJC ELEMENTS

applied to the situation and/or issue will increase joy by acting differently next time with

cognitive intention. I am committed to applying the element(s) above next-time the issue arises.

I'm responsible for my behavior and how it relates to The Joy Codex and increasing joy.

BWWBR0006.0   www.thejoycodex.com   Codex Capstone Media L.L.C.

The Joy Codex Thoughts, Emotions, Behaviors Worksheet

THOUGHTS, EMOTIONS, BEHAVIORS WORKSHEET				
Name::		Date:		
Today I thought	POSITIVELY/NEGATIVELY CIRCLE ONE	about	SELF/OTHER CIRCLE ONE	Specifically,
I tought				
	YOUR THOUGHTS			
	YOUR THOUGHTS CONTINUED			
Then I felt				
	YOUR EMOTIONS			
	YOUR EMOTIONS CONTINUED			
I behaved with				
	YOUR SPECIFIC ACTIONS AS A RESULT OF THOUGHTS			
	YOUR SPECIFIC ACTIONS AS A RESULT OF THOUGHTS CONTINUED			
My behavior was	POSITIVE/NEGATIVE CIRCLE ONE	My Thoughts increased my joy	YES/NO CIRCLE ONE	IF NO –
	WHAT WILL YOU REPLACE YOUR NEGETIVE THOUGHTS WITH? LIST NEW SPECIFIC THOUGHTS			
WHAT WILL YOU REPLACE YOUR NEGETIVE THOUGHTS WITH? LIST NEW SPECIFIC THOUGHTS CONTINUED				

BWWBR0007.0   www.thejoycodex.com   Codex Capstone Media L.L.C.

The Thoughts, Emotions, Behaviors Worksheet is designed to get your brain making the automatic connection to Thoughts → Emotions → Behaviors. If your thoughts are negative, this form will help you replace the negative thoughts for positive thoughts, leading to positive emotions and behavior.

EXAMPLE

THOUGHTS, EMOTIONS, BEHAVIORS WORKSHEET EXAMPLE			
Name::		Date:	

Today I thought	POSITIVELY/**NEGATIVELY**	about	**SELF**/OTHER	Specifically,
	CIRCLE ONE		CIRCLE ONE	

I thought	that I wasn't good enough for a new project that needed a leader.
YOUR THOUGHTS	

YOUR THOUGHTS CONTINUED	
Then I felt	insecure and incapabale as an employee and that my skillset wasn't good enough.
YOUR EMOTIONS	

YOUR EMOTIONS CONTINUED	
I behaved with	not deciding to offer to lead the project.
YOUR SPECIFIC ACTIONS AS A RESULT OF THOUGHTS	

YOUR SPECIFIC ACTIONS AS A RESULT OF THOUGHTS CONTINUED			
My behavior was	POSITIVE/**NEGATIVE**	My thoughts increased my joy	YES/**NO**	IF NO --
	CIRCLE ONE		CIRCLE ONE	

I will replace my negative thoughts of not being qualified as a project leader with thoughts of confidence knowing that I have

WHAT WILL YOU REPLACE YOUR NEGETIVE THOUGHTS WITH? LIST NEW SPECIFIC THOUGHTS

lead new projects in the past with great success. I KNOW I am qualified and will do an excellent job.

WHAT WILL YOU REPLACE YOUR NEGETIVE THOUGHTS WITH? LIST NEW SPECIFIC THOUGHTS CONTINUED

BWWBR0007.0   www.thejoycodex.com   Codex Capstone Media L.L.C. ©

The Joy Codex Change My Thoughts, Emotions, Behaviors Worksheet

CHANGE MY THOUGHTS, EMOTIONS, BEHAVIORS WORKSHEET	
Name:	Date:
Today I want to think positively about SELF/OTHER/SITUATION CIRCLE ONE	Specifically, I want to think LIST THE POSITIVE THOUGHTS
LIST THE POSITIVE THOUGHTS CONTINUED	
LIST THE POSITIVE THOUGHTS CONTINUED	
These new positive thoughts specific to SELF/OTHER/SITUATION CIRCLE ONE	are intended to increase my emotions / feelings of
LIST THE POSITIVE EMOTIONS INTENDED	
My emotions will influence my specific behavior LIST YOUR DESIRED BEHAVIOR	
LIST YOUR DESIRED BEHAVIOR CONTINUED	

PART 2

At the end of the day, please reflect on your behavior. determine how your thoughts influenced your emotions and behavior

Were you able to replace your negative thoughts with positive thoughts? YES/NO CIRCLE ONE   Your thoughts influence your emotions.

Did your thoughts influence your emotions? YES/NO CIRCLE ONE   Did you get the results you expected? YES/NO CIRCLE ONE

If you didn't get the results you expected what will you do differently? ACTIONS YOU WILL TAKE

BWWBR008.3 www.thejoycodex.com

The Change My Thoughts, Emotions, Behaviors Worksheet is designed to replace specific negative thoughts, emotions, behaviors about self, others, or a situation in advance of that event. Example, I have a meeting later today and I want to think positively about the situation, therefore I am choosing to think positively knowing that my positive thoughts increase my positive emotion and behavior. Another two examples, today I want to increase my positive internal dialogue or today I want to increase my positive thoughts about another. This form you get you prepared to change your negative thoughts with specific actions that lead to positive thoughts.

EXAMPLE

CHANGE MY THOUGHTS, EMOTIONS, BEHAVIORS WORKSHEET **EXAMPLE**		

Name: _Scot Gorman_   Date: _10/5/2019_

Today I want to think positively about   SELF/OTHER/**SITUATION**   Specifically, I want to think   _positively about a meeting_
CIRCLE ONE   LIST THE POSITIVE THOUGHTS

I have coming up this week with my boss about a project I am working on. I am confident about the time I have spent on the project
LIST THE POSITIVE THOUGHTS CONTINUED

having a positive impact. I did all the research and am well versed in the project subject. I can speak to the subject.
LIST THE POSITIVE THOUGHTS CONTINUED

These new positive thoughts specific to   SELF/OTHER/**SITUATION**   are intended to increase my emotions / feelings of
CIRCLE ONE

confidence, well-being, satisfaction, enthusiasm, contentment, and joy.
LIST THE POSITIVE EMOTIONS INTENDED

My emotions will influence my specific behavior   _I want to attend the meeting with my boss and be clear and concise about my work when_
LIST YOUR DESIRED BEHAVIOR

speaking with my boss. I want to be assertive and demonstrate that my bosses confidence in me is warranted.
LIST YOUR DESIRED BEHAVIOR CONTINUED

PART 2
At the end of the day, please reflect on your behavior. determine how your thoughts influenced your emotions and behavior
Were you able to replace your negative thoughts with positive thoughts?   **YES**/NO   Your thoughts influence your emotions.
CIRCLE ONE
Did your thoughts influence your emotions?   **YES**/NO   Did you get the results you expected?   **YES**/NO
CIRCLE ONE   CIRCLE ONE

If you didn't get the results you expected what will you do differently?
BWWBR0083 www.thejoycodex.com   ACTIONS YOU WILL TAKE

ABOUT THE AUTHOR

Scot Gorman is the author and creator of The Joy Codex, he lives in Orange County, California. The Joy Codex was developed over many years with influences from his professional experience and his experience with CBT/DBT, Performance Management, and Six Sigma. Join him on a journey of self-discovery and spiritual reawakening. The Joy Codex is a set of principles he developed and shared over his lifetime that have worked for him and others. Having joy shouldn't be a luxury, joy should be simple enough to achieve daily.